BRITISH COLUMBIA
Vancouver

GW00708348

APA PUBLICATIONS **L**

Part of the Langenscheidt Publishing Group

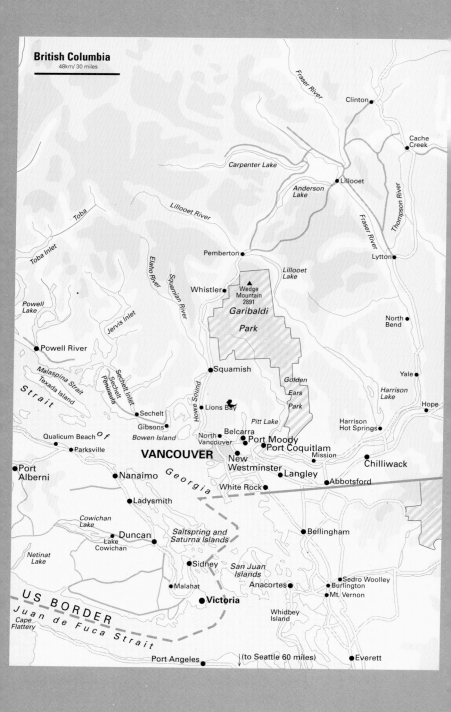

Welcome!

There can be few cities in the world that are so urbane yet so cradled in wilderness as Vancouver, where mountain peaks loom above grand boulevards and there are sudden glimpses of sunlit water glistening between skyscraper buildings. It is a youthful city, built by immigrants, a place which loves innovation yet is still guided by a pioneer spirit. All of this is reflected in Vancouver's unconventional architecture, its historic downtown centre, its ethnic neighbourhoods, its international cuisine, its wealth of outdoor activities and its considerable number of museums.

In these pages, Insight's specialist on British Columbia, Joel Rogers, has designed three full-day itineraries, incorporating what he considers to be the most outstanding sights. In addition, seven Pick & Mix half-day itineraries will help you discover and appreciate all the varied aspects of the city, and for those with time to venture further afield there are three suggested excursions – to the picturesque streets of Victoria, to the idyllic Gulf Islands and to Whistler Mountain, with its year-round sporting activities. Supporting the itineraries are sections on history and culture, eating out, nightlife and practical information, including recommended hotels.

 Joel W Rogers is a freelance writer and photographer who has long specialized in assignments on the Northwest coast of North America. Each visit he made to British Columbia made him feel more and more at home there, until finally he gave in and moved to the area of Vancouver called Kitsilano, across English Bay from the West End. He promptly threw himself into the life of the city and has never looked back. We believe that the enthusiasm he feels for British Columbia, with its invigorating mixture of the unexpected and the traditional, as well as the fun he had in finding out about it, is reflected in the following pages, and we hope that it will communicate itself to you.

C O N T E N T S

Pages 2/3:
Kitsilano Beach

Excursions

Pages 8/9:
Canadian giants

Shopping, Dining & Nightlife

Calendar of Events

Practical Information

Maps

HISTORY &

Captain George Vancouver pacing the quarterdeck as the natives approached in cedar canoes is a romantic beginning for a city. But the arrival of His Majesty's ships in 1792 – embellished to form a boaster's tale of intrepid mariners, fur trappers and gold prospectors – is not where this history begins. The origins and currents of this city run 10,000 years deeper. The land that now supports a diverse population of 2.5 million has long been home to bands of people, known collectively as the Northwest Coast people, who arrived by land bridge from Asia, migrating south both along the coast and down the ice-free corridors of the interior, to settle in the delta and the inlet that would become the city of Vancouver.

The People of the Grass

Throughout the broken and intricate fjords to the north and the broad-beached alluvial plains to the south, the people built their villages. Free from the ever-present threat of scarcity that plagued the natives of the plains and prairies, the Coast peoples had time to create their art, their inventions and their legends, and to develop what some anthropologists consider the richest culture of all the hunting peoples of the world.

Two dominant bands shared what is now Vancouver. The Musqueam, 'the people of the grass', built along the salt-grass margins of the Fraser river delta. The Squamish lived on the north shores of Burrard Inlet and in their northern winter villages at the windy head of Howe Sound, giving them their name, 'strong winds'. By all accounts the bands lived in relative harmony with their neighbours, they had summer homes and vacations, and held lavish entertainments, known as *potlatches*.

Carved out of history

Culture

We Called them Men-O-War

It may have been a Musqueam band which in 1791 welcomed the Spanish explorer Don José Maria Narvaez, as his 11-m (36-ft) schooner stood off Point Grey. A year later Captain George Vancouver on his epic voyage in search of the Northwest Passage would sail the ship *Discovery* through the first narrows and into history.

Vancouver's landing

Between 1792, when Captain Vancouver charted Burrard Inlet, and 1851, when gold was discovered on the Fraser, British Columbia became a crown colony. The power and the population of the Musqueam and Squamish dwindled with the establishment of Hudson Bay's Fort Langley and New Westminster up the Fraser river. By 1862, devastating smallpox epidemics had wiped out two-thirds of the British Columbia bands (or 80,000 people). Those who remained were excluded from the new province's rights and power.

The Finest Trees in the World

It wasn't gold that made the white man settle British Columbia, however, it was timber. George Vancouver noted in his log, 'Well covered with trees of large growth principally of the pine tribe'. Remarkable trees, firs as high as contemporary Vancouver's tallest buildings, were perfect for the masts of the Royal Navy's ships. In the 1860s, the navy designated a number of reserves around Burrard Inlet to supply masts for its ships.

Living in the perpetual shade of fir, hemlock, spruce and cedar trees, the first settlers chopped out clearings and learned to girdle and to burn the massive trees until they fell. Loggers fed the mills, and the entire region became a perpetual haze of slash burning as

J. A. BROCK, Portrait and Landscape Photographer, BRANDON, MAN., AND VANCOUVER, CITY.

Felling the giants

the virgin rain forest was steadily cut beyond the tiny settlements along the inlet.

By 1870 the Vancouver-to-be was a 11-ha (28-acre), 50-inhabitant, two-block-long string of wood frame houses, hotels, and four saloons. The locals named it Gastown after the loquacious 'Gassy' Jack Deighton, founder and proprietor of the city's first 'watering hole'. Here gold miners of the Caribou mixed with ships' hands and loggers from the camps. Most people spoke Chinook, a Native trade language, in part because the newcomers were Russian, Chilean, Kanakan (Hawaiian), Portuguese, Belgian, French, Spanish, Finnish, Austrian and American.

In 1884 Gastown, renamed Granville, still two blocks long, changed its name to Vancouver at the suggestion of William Van Horne, the general manager of the Canadian Pacific Railroad. Along with the name, everything changed. More than 500 buildings rose up, as people anticipated the new railhead. Thousands of men laboured, property repeatedly changed hands, the dirt streets were extended, and the forests razed until one Sunday afternoon – on 13 June 1886 – it all burned down.

In one hour, an out-of-control slash fire swept through the streets, forcing people into Burrard Inlet and False Creek with just the clothes on their back. There was no fighting it; the town was gone. But within a year the people rebuilt the city on a firmer and finer footing, and on 23 May 1887, the eve of Queen Victoria's birthday, welcomed the first transcontinental train.

The Train to the Future

With the arrival of the first train, the future of the region began to take shape. Vancouver was already destined to be Canada's western port city: no other coastal port had both the route through British Columbia's mountainous topography and a deep-water harbour. With the railroad link, the most beautiful steamships the world

12

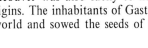

New arrivals

has ever seen — the Canadian Pacific's *Empresses* — began shipping raw silk and tea across the North Pacific. Canada's Pacific Rim trade came of age. Both the area and the company began to grow rich.

Vancouver also benefitted greatly from the reign of the Canadian Pacific Railroad, as this Montreal-based company orchestrated amenities a frontier city could never command. Vancouver was also lucky to have townspeople with international origins. The inhabitants of Gastown hailed from every corner of the world and sowed the seeds of today's uniquely cosmopolitan city.

A City of Immigrants

This was not without pain. The Chinese, Japanese, and East Indian immigrants and the Native Peoples were all persecuted and excluded throughout the early history of the city.

Between 1881 and 1885, 17,000 Chinese came to British Columbia to work on the railroad, to mine (they at one time constituted three-quarters of the miners on the Cariboo gold fields), to fill the canneries on the coast, and to serve in the kitchens of almost every substantial house from Victoria to Vancouver. Alarmed by the surging populations of 'orientals', the province and the federal government passed the Chinese Immigration Act of 1885, the first of many laws that would deny Asians the right to vote, to lease crown land or to choose their professions.

The Japanese began arriving in numbers after 1896. They pioneered the herring fisheries and exported dog salmon to Japan. They worked the mills and farms, and opened shops and stores around the 200 block of Powell Street.

By the 1890s the Musqueams and Squamish, torn between their ancient ways of seasonal food gathering and the new-found wealth at the mills and canneries, saw the fabric of their lives begin to unravel. Relegated to a few Indian reserves, their concept of territory, family fish camps and sacred sites was superseded by European deeds, surveys and ownership, their way of life undermined by European attempts to impose alien values upon them.

Haida Indians

A Coming of Age

At the turn of the century Vancouver began the greatest growth period of its history. It had already become the financial, transportation and supply center of British Columbia. Now mining expanded into copper, lead and zinc; coal remained number one, and gold production tripled. Forty-nine salmon canneries operated on the Fraser. The wheat farmers of the prairies swallowed up three-quarters of British Columbia's lumber production; and the new market for pulp and paper created 100 new forestry companies in 10 years.

From 1910–12 the population of the city quadrupled from 27,000 to 122,000. The city limits expanded from 4sq km (1½sq miles) to 35sq km (13½sq miles), as grand buildings rose to shadow Gastown. The Dominion Trust soared to thirteen storeys in 1909, but was quickly topped by newspaper publisher Louis B Taylor's 17-storey Sun-World Tower, the tallest buildings in the British Empire. Sidewalks were still wood, and the roads were either brick, macadam or mud. Cars began to appear, but the streetcars carried most people to work on 400km (250 miles) of new track.

New neighbourhoods began to take shape; immigrants moved into Strathcona, Grandview and East Hastings. Downtown office workers built in Kitsilano and Dunbar, those on the social register moved into in Point Grey, Kerrisdale and Shaughnessy Heights.

Vancouver's natural beaches were purchased: English Bay and Kitsilano first, with Jericho and Spanish Banks to follow. The University of British Columbia was sited on the government reserve at Point Grey. At that time 72 percent of Vancouver's business leaders had only a high school education, and the majority of Vancouverites were immigrants – one-third of them British. In 1912 Mary Henrietta McNaughton was elected to the school board, becoming the first woman to gain office in the city. When World War I began 28,000 Vancouver men and women enlisted – this was the highest proportion from just one North America city to be sent to the trenches of France.

Vancouver c1930

A Trolly to the Suburbs

By the end of the war Vancouver had settled down as a city of wage earners. And though the economy cooled off, the town matured, becoming the first Canadian city to adopt comprehensive zoning laws, while new commercial strips followed the trolly tracks into the suburbs. More parks and six golf courses came into being, and there was skiing at Grouse Mountain. The area was beginning to play. But then the Depression hit.

Dependent upon its export-based industries, Vancouver reeled from layoffs and bankruptcies. Nearly one-third of the population was out of work in 1936, while the city foreclosed on 31,000 properties for non-payment of taxes. The areas of North Vancouver and Burnaby went bankrupt. It would take World War II to return the city to prosperity.

The war years began with the internment of the Japanese citizens — 9,000 in Vancouver alone, their property sold at auction at roughly ten cents on the dollar. At the same time, *Japanese internment*

skilled immigrants and refugees who had been relegated to farm labour during peacetime became crucial to the retooling for war. Women went to work as never before, 60,000 strong in the city's shipyards, mills, and businesses.

A Post-War Populace

The post-war years' growth was as explosive as that at the beginning of the century. The suburbs doubled in population, and the British flavour of the city began to blend into an international stew as refugees from Europe and Asia flooded the province. The Commonwealth Games held in Vancouver in 1954 put the city on the world stage. The era of the street car ended just as Vancouver began to feel big-city pressures. Traffic was building, and no solutions were in sight. The West End was entirely re-zoned for high-rise apartments; plans were afoot for the 'urban renewal' of Chinatown and Strathcona. In October 1967 plans for the first of 14 freeways, a major connector through the heart of Chinatown, were unveiled, but community protest and high costs caused the planners' retreat. No freeway has been built within Vancouver proper, making it the only major North American city without one.

By 1970 the great influx of post-war immigrants had turned many neighbourhoods into celebrated ethnic communities. With 10,000 Italian-born residents centred around Commercial Street, the Greeks on Fourth, 8,000 Germans calling Robson Street 'Robsonstrasse', not to mention the well-established Chinatown enriched by the influx of 15,000 people from Hong Kong and Taiwan, the character of the city became decidedly international.

The Saltwater City

Citizens of Vancouver

Expo '86, an exposition to celebrate Vancouver's 100th birthday, thrust the region into the international limelight. Expo '86 covered one-tenth of the downtown core and built a monument to the future. With transportation as its primary theme, it was a resounding success. Expo funded Vancouver's first light-rail 'Sky-Train', and built Canada Place, but the most profound and lasting effect was the raising of the Pacific Northwest's image on the international horizon.

In the aftermath of Expo '86, Hong Kong multi-billionaire Li Ka-shing purchased the entire site (204 acres for $125 million, considered the 'deal of the century'), causing the whole international financial community to take notice. No one is certain how much international investment is flowing into Vancouver, but it is obvious that the city is prospering and changing. Li Ka-shing's buildings are just springing up and the single-family home in Vancouver is becoming an endangered species, due to rapidly rising costs.

Tung Chan, investment banker and past city alderman, thinks the financial future of the region is secure, 'The framework is in place for Vancouver to be the international financial and maritime gateway between the Pacific Rim and North America' he says. Vancouver is rapidly becoming its own version of Hong Kong, but it is the people, not the finance, who have made Saltwater City what it is today. It is they who will ensure its future, and the city which gave birth to Greenpeace, one of the most effective environmental organisations in the world, will always be aware of environmental considerations and the importance of ensuring a good quality of life for its diverse mixture of citizens.

Vancouver's changing face

Historical Highlights

8000BC–present Earliest findings of the Northwest Coast people settling along the shores of the Fraser River.

500BC Earliest dates of inhabitation within Vancouver proper at Ee'yullmough Village at Jericho Beach.

1791 Spanish navigator José Maria Navárez enters Burrard Inlet.

1792 Captain George Vancouver claims the region for Great Britain.

1827 Fort Langley, a Hudson's Bay fur-trade outpost, is built on the south shore of the Fraser.

1850 British Columbia native population down to 60,000 from an estimated 150,000 in 1770s due largely to smallpox.

1851 Gold discovered on the Fraser drainage bringing 22,000 miners, including the region's first Chinese residents. Great Britain proclaims the territory the 'Colony of British Columbia'.

1864 The first lumber export, 277,500 board feet of fir, is loaded aboard the barque *Ellen Lewis* bound for Adelaide, in Australia. Governor Douglas creates Indian reserves.

1867 Jack Deighton builds a saloon to become the centre of 'Gastown'.

1872 The provincial government amends the Voter Act to exclude Chinese and Native residents.

1884 Floating salmon-cannery refuse blamed on fish die-off in Coal Harbour: Vancouver's first pollution alert.

1886 Vancouver's 1,000 buildings burn to the ground in an hour and are rebuilt within one year. The City of Granville becomes the City of Vancouver. Lauchlan Hamilton, CPR's civil engineer, proposes Stanley Park.

1887 The first CPR transcontinental and steamship service is joined in Vancouver, linking the Orient to Europe in 29 days.

1890s The first golf course west of the Mississippi is laid out at Jericho about the time the first suburb, Mount Pleasant, is planned.

1914–18 Vancouver sends a higher proportion of soldiers to France than any other North American city.

1920s Wreck Beach at Point Grey becomes known for its clothing-optional bathing.

1929 British Columbia has 4,000 logging operations and 350 mills.

1937 Strathcona Elementary School teaches students who represent 57 nationalities.

1947–8 Asian and Native residents granted vote in provincial, and later national, elections.

1952 Diners can now have a drink with their food.

1967 Vancouverites found the environmental group Greenpeace, which later becomes international.

1974 Eight forestry companies control 82 percent of British Columbia's harvesting rights.

1978 An estimated 50 percent of Vancouver's prime office and apartment buildings are owned by Hong Kong interests.

1986 Expo '86 draws 22 million visitors and establishes Vancouver as an international tourist and trade destination.

1992 Vancouver-born Kim Campbell becomes British Columbia's first Prime Minister of Canada.

1993 Average detached house price in Vancouver reaches $500,000; in the region: $350,000.

1999 Population of Vancouver approaches 2 million, with a growth rate of twice the national average and 84 percent of new immigrants arriving from countries in Asia.

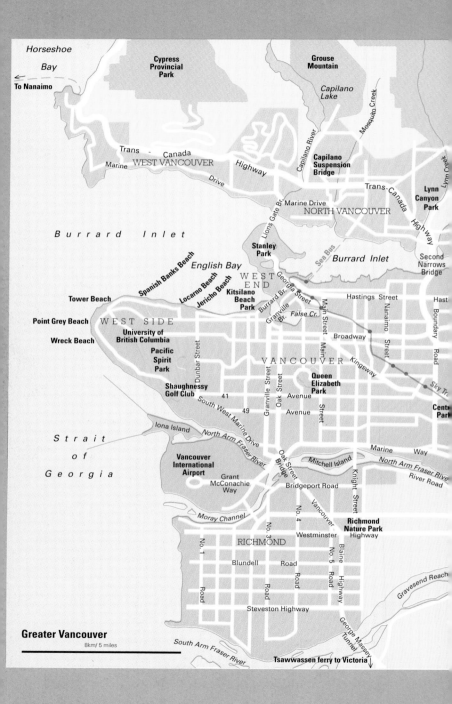

Horseshoe Bay

To Nanaimo

Cypress Provincial Park

Grouse Mountain

Capilano Lake

Mosquito Creek

Lynn Creek

Capilano River

Capilano Suspension Bridge

Trans - Canada Highway
Marine Drive
WEST VANCOUVER
Highway

Lions Gate Br.

Trans-Canada Highway

Lynn Canyon Park

Marine Drive
NORTH VANCOUVER

Second Narrows Bridge

B u r r a r d   I n l e t

Stanley Park

Sea Bus

Burrard Inlet

English Bay

WEST END

Spanish Banks Beach

Locarno Beach

Jericho Beach

Kitsilano Beach Park

Tower Beach

WEST SIDE

Georgia Street

Hastings Street

Hast

Burrard Br.

Granville Br.

False Cr.

Main Street

Nanaimo Street

Boundary Road

Point Grey Beach

Wreck Beach

University of British Columbia

Broadway

Pacific Spirit Park

Dunbar Street

VANCOUVER

Main

Kingsway

Sky Tr.

Shaughnessy Golf Club

Granville Street

Oak Street

Queen Elizabeth Park

Street

Cent Park

41

South West Marine Drive

49

Avenue

Avenue

S t r a i t

o f

G e o r g i a

Iona Island

North Arm Fraser River

Marine   Way

Mitchell Island

North Arm Fraser Rive

River Road

Vancouver International Airport

Grant McConachie Way

Oak Street Bridge

Bridgeport Road

Knight Street

Vancouver

Moray Channel

No. 4

Richmond Nature Park

No. 3

RICHMOND

Westminster

No. 5

Blaine

Highway

Highway

Blundell   Road

Road

Road

No. 1

Road

Road

Gravesend Reach

Steveston Highway

George Massey Tunnel

Greater Vancouver

8km/ 5 miles

South Arm Fraser River

Tsawwassen ferry to Victoria

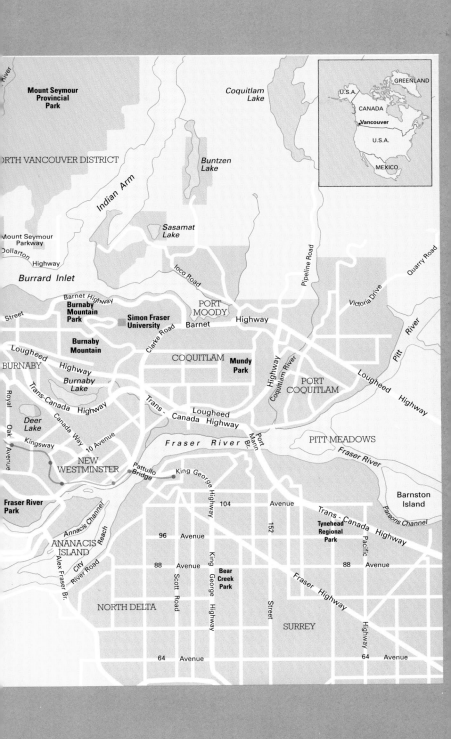

Day Itinerary

DAY (1)

The Heart of the City: Downtown to Gastown

Take a leisurely walk through the heart of Vancouver and let the pace and the people tell you about this city. Art, business, history, culture and cuisine all converge in the urban forest, and this itinerary introduces you to its unconventional architecture, to the Vancouver Art Gallery, the Canadian Craft Museum, to some great hotels and ocean liners; and takes you around historic Gastown.

—Vancouver's downtown is a compact one, the walking is easy and relatively short-distanced. Check the weather and bring sun glasses even when it looks like rain. Plan on breakfast along the way, and make dinner reservations as soon as possible from the suggestions at the end of today's itinerary—

Dressed for fun

The business, hotel and department-store district of Vancouver is bustling, healthy, surprisingly quiet, clean and fun. It is smart and young, expensive and bohemian, with an attractive and polite populace who wait at the traffic lights and dote on pedestrians. It is as comfortable and safe an urban centre as you'll ever experience.

Begin your day at **Robson Square** on Robson Street between Hornby and Howe

streets and walk south into the square, up the wave of stairs to the highest point, then turn: around you is Vancouver's architecture, which few cities can match. To the west **Cathedral Place** (924 West Georgia Street at Hornby Street), designed by Paul Merrick, compliments the copper-roofed landmark Canadian Pacific **Hotel Vancouver**. To the east is, as one architect put it, the 'ghastly' but busy **Eatons** department store. In the centre is the old court house that now houses the extensive **Vancouver Art Gallery** (Monday, Wednesday, Friday, Saturday 10am–5pm, Thursday 10am–9pm, Sunday noon–5pm). Behind you are the new **Courts of Justice**, designed by the internationally famous local architect Arthur Erickson.

Now for breakfast. Finding a good breakfast restaurant among the underground-mall muffin shops and entree-priced hotel menus takes luck and persistence. On the west side of Hornby Street there are a number that are comfy, sunlit (hopefully) and good: the best is the **Bacchus Ristorante and Lounge** at the **Wedgewood Hotel**, 845 Hornby, \$\$, one of Vancouver's best hotels and nicest streetside settings. Or head north (towards the water) to the Hotel Vancouver's **Griffins**, \$\$. In Cathedral Place are two options: the 'open at 6.10am' **My Honey's Buns**, \$, has espresso and baked goods, and down the interior hall towards the Canadian Craft Museum is **Garden Deli**, \$. Dawdle over breakfast with the *Globe and Mail* or the *National Post*, Canada's equivalent to the British *Times*.

Robson Square

Canadian craftwork

Return to the street for a brief lesson in civic and corporate sculptures. At **Cathedral Place** look up to see the terra cotta griffins and 'nurses', recasts from the controversial destruction of the earlier Georgia Medical Dental Building. Across Hornby Street at the **Hong Kong Bank of Canada**, in the enclosed atrium, is **The Pendulum** by Alan Storey, guaranteed to mystify. Across Georgia Street is Count Alex Von Svoboda's **Centennial Fountain**, with its bronze faces of Celtic origin.

Access to the **Vancouver Art Gallery**, Georgia and Howe Streets, tel: 662 4700, is at the side of the building. Start at the top of the three floors and spend up to two hours enjoying both the permanent and the travelling shows. Take particular note of the **Emily Carr** collection – more than 40 works by British Columbia's best-known painter that capture the haunting mysticism of the First Peoples, particularly the Haida of the Queen Charlotte Islands. When leaving the museum browse in the gift shop: it's at the museums that you'll find some of the city's best books and gifts.

Back on Hornby Street, walk north to Cathedral Place and visit the **Canadian Craft Museum** (Monday to Saturday 9.30am–5.30pm, Sunday noon–5pm). Within this state-of-the-art space is an ongoing collection of Canada's world-respected art form – crafts of remarkable imagination and impact.

Marine Building

You can lunch early at **Garden Deli** and sit out in the courtyard adjoining the museum – a favourite enclave of the office crowd – or continue down Hornby Street. Crossing West Hastings Street look left at the 1930s art deco **Marine Building**, long the symbol of Vancouver's emergence as a city. Through its arched, ornate entrance is a lobby of encrusted terracotta ornamentation, a monument to Vancouver's maritime presence.

Hornby Street meets the sea at the futuristic silver-and-white **Canada Place,** built for Expo '86, the world exposition that put Vancouver on the international map. It now serves the **Port of Vancouver's** thriving cruise-ship trade, embarking more than half a million people on 20 Alaska-bound ocean liners every week from mid-May to mid-September. Walk along the west promenade for a close look at these great ships. Holland America's **MV Westerdam** – which weighs 52,000 tonnes, measures 243m (798ft) in length

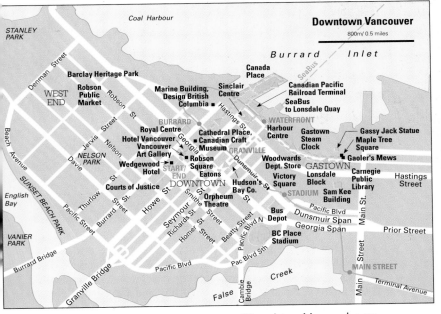

and carries 1,494 passengers – or one of her sister ships, arrive every Tuesday, Thursday, Saturday and every second Sunday, docking at 7am and departing at 5.45pm.

Once you've reached the end of the pier take the stairs across the front, passing – or stopping to enjoy seafood at – the **Prow Restaurant**, tel: 684 1339, $$. Then continue up to the northeast end of the pier to where plaques tell of the history and energy of the Port of Vancouver. The view is sweeping. It is a wonderful way to look at the harbour and is also for anchoring your sense of direction.

Turn and walk the east side of the pier to Cordova Street and cross to enter the **Sinclair Centre**, which has imaginatively preserved four remarkable buildings joined by a covered atrium. There is shopping and a variety of fast lunch restaurants. Pass through, heading east, and regain Cordova Street by entering the **Waterfront Station**, site of the 1887 completion of the trans-Canada national railway, which is now a terminal for the **Sky Train** and the **SeaBus**.

History now colours your day as you turn left and into the site of Vancouver's first European settlement, known as **Gastown**. In 1867 'Portuguese Joe' ran the general store and 'Gassy' Jack Deighton built a tavern with a barrel of whisky. Today Gastown is a tree-lined Vic-

Street entertainment

Gastown's steam clock

torian business and shopping district that still echoes the free-wheeling days of the pioneers. A logical starting point is **The Landing** (Water and Cordova Streets), once home to a wholesale grocery firm specializing in catering for gold prospectors. Then take the left side of **Water Street** and browse. The **Inuit Gallery** at 345 Water Street is one of the best First Nations art galleries. At the **La Luna Café** is one of the most beautiful signs in the city, and inside is serious coffee. The world's first steam clock greets you with the notes of Big Ben (every 15 minutes). Cross over to the **Edward Hotel Building**, dating from 1906. Here you can enjoy a good late lunch either outdoors or in one of the dining rooms where plenty of windows give light and space.

Lovely La Luna

At **Maple Tree Square** note the statue of 'Gassy Jack', standing on a barrel, and along Carrall Street the increasingly residential Gastown, a new concept in this renaissance neighbourhood. Turn back and go into **Gaoler's Mews** off Maple Tree Square, an old stable yard and one of the most intriguing spaces in the city. It was the sight of Gastown's first police station, and is now a brick-floored alley with ivy-covered walls and a musical carousel clock. Prisoners in ankle chains were once used as labour on road-cleaning projects; perhaps that is where **Blood Alley Square**, the cobbled yard behind the mews, gets its name from. Note the offices of Paul Merrick, who was the architect of Cathedral Place.

Back on Water Street, return on the city side and explore the labyrinth of restaurants, shops and work spaces. Antique shops and vintage clothing stores sell wares from bygone eras, and native galleries and souvenir shops are plentiful.

Back at the intersection of Water and Cordova streets you're on your own. Take a cab back to the hotel or walk the short eight blocks leading southwest to Robson Square. Along the way you'll find exquisite fountain pens at the **Vancouver Pen Shop Ltd**, 512 West Hastings Street.

Finish the day with a quiet drink and a sweeping view in the **Roof Lounge** at the top of the **Hotel Vancouver**, 900 Georgia Street. Dinner suggestions? My choice of restaurant is **Le Crocodile**, 909 Burrard, entrance on Smithe, tel: 669 4298, $$$, a warm, rich location with an Alsace-inspired menu. Other options include the following: **Chartwell**, Four Seasons Hotel, 791 West Georgia Street, tel: 689 9333, $$$, the restaurant that fluctuates between traditional and contemporary and has enjoyed some great reviews. **Joe Fortes Seafood and Chop House**, 777 Thurlow Street, tel: 669 1940, $$, is a scene, also with an oyster bar – sometimes with New Orleans jazz – and always attracts a crowd, especially on Friday and Saturday nights. **Phnom Penh**, 244 East Georgia Street, tel: 682 5777, $, serves Cambodian, Vietnamese and Chinese cuisine to simple perfection. Try starting with the sweet-and-sour soups and garlic-fried squid.

Stanley Park and the West End

Take a walking tour of Stanley Park's evergreen forests, seaside paths, mountain views, beaches and gardens. Visits the Vancouver Zoo and Aquarium and the Variety Kids Water Park. Have a Teahouse lunch, then cross the street to a different kind of forest – the high-rise delights of the West End. End the day strolling Denman and Robson streets and eating well.

–Our starting point is Robson Square. This is a walking day with taxi or bus assistance if required. For those who like to walk or rent bicycles, dress accordingly. Pack a fresh shirt for the casually dressy Teahouse Restaurant, 2099 Beach Avenue, tel: 669 3281 (brunch or lunch until 2.15pm). For dinner, try Delilah's, 1789 Comox Street, tel: 687 3424 (no reservations) or CinCin Ristorante, 1154 Robson Street, tel: 688 7338–

Imagine a frontier of nothing but trees: a solid wall of evergreens up to 90m (300ft) high confronting the Vancouver pioneers. They burned them, girdled them and sold

Old growth and new cars

Starbucks

them for a dollar apiece – just to see the sky. By 1889 what little remained of the forest within the growing city limits was a military reserve, a peninsula at the mouth of Burrard Inlet – 440ha (1,000 acres) of cool, green firs, meadow and beach that, by luck and foresight, became **Stanley Park**. Larger than New York's Central Park, dedicated by Lord Stanley, Governor General of Canada, only three years after the 1886 incorporation of the city, it is one of the finest parks in the world. To get a full appreciation of this urban wilderness we are going to walk, if not all the way around the park's 8-km (5-mile) perimeter, then at least to some of its most interesting shoreline and forest trails.

Walking down **Robson Street** from **Robson Square**, the tall firs and cedars become visible through the steel and concrete canyons of the West End. Take the west side of Robson Street and window shop through a trendy, touristy set of store fronts and cafés. **Duthie Books**, 919 Robson Street, is a venerable Vancouver establishment. A string of high-fashion or chic boutiques, lofts, little restaurants, casual cafés, jewelry stores and souvenir stores form an eclectic array. Then, dodging not one but two **Starbucks** coffee houses at Robson and Thurlow streets, choose one of the many java houses to satisfy your caffeine craving – cappuccino with wonderful opportunities for people-watching. For breakfast without an attitude try the **Bread Garden**, 812 Bute Street, $ (a half block south of Robson Street). It has fast, take-a-number, 24-hour service and freshly baked goods.

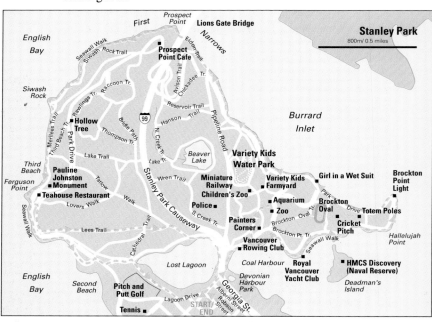

Boats and buildings

Fortified, return to Robson and walk down the hill. Though quiet in the morning, this is one of the most popular streets to stroll in the city: the sidewalks are crowded with all ages, restaurants are five to ten a block, and European- and American-style hotels flank and encroach the street's shop-and-awning ambiance. As you approach Denman you can rent bikes or roller blades from a number of rental shops. Everything is provided at **Bayshore Bicycles and Rollerblade Rentals**, 745 Denman Street, tel: 688 2453.

Walking, riding or rolling, continue on Robson Street to Chilco Street. Take a right, passing the park's bus station. (At weekends there is a **No 52 Round the Park bus** that circles the park every hour; you can get on and off again at your whim.) Passing the station, take the tunnel beneath busy Highway 99 to the seawall and turn left (walkers on the right) to begin your day's exploration of Stanley Park.

On the water side is the 1911 Tudor-style **Vancouver Rowing Club** and the yachts of the **Royal Vancouver Yacht Club**. Through the masts and rigging the city comes into view. You can take some of your best photographs of the city right here, and most people do. Just beyond the rowing club there's a parking lot with an information booth. Get a free map of the park – very important or we'll lose you in the woods!

If you choose to visit the diminutive **Vancouver Zoo** and the extensive **Vancouver Aquarium** (July and August 9.30am–8pm, winter 10am–5.30pm; tel: 268 9900), continue through the parking lot up into the trees a short distance. The zoo is more of a habitat preserve with little to see. But at least it's free. Right in its heart look up to see a wild, great blue heron rookery with nesting herons in the summer. From there you have the choice of the fun **Children's Farmyard** and also the **Stanley Park Junction** miniature railway up to the left, or the aquarium to the right.

The **Vancouver Aquarium** is a walk-through of British Columbia's marine environments, tropical and Amazonian galleries with piranha, caimans, and rain storms with real rain. But the captivating feature of the aquarium is the whales – glistening

Pedalling through the pines

Otter's photocall

black Orcas and snow-white Belugas in open-air pools you can view from the surface or below through tank-long windows. The aquarium no longer trains these exceptionally intelligent and social mammals to entertain, due in part to the growing public interest in freeing the whales. Nonetheless, it is fascinating to be so close to such beautiful living beings.

From the aquarium check your map, go back to the seawall and turn left to a **thicket of totem poles** representing the collected bands of British Columbia's Native American people. These valuable poles were saved from destruction in the period between 1900 and 1950 when totems were not esteemed. Today they are carefully preserved. The individual poles, though beautiful, are not described.

Continue around the seawall to **Brockton Point** for a look at the city, the harbour and North Vancouver. (The bright yellow pile among the freighters is sulphur.) At 3km (1½ miles) – painted markers are along the base of the seawall curb – is Vancouver's artistically whimsical takeoff of Copenhagen's *Little Mermaid* called *Girl in a Wetsuit* (though this statue is clearly a two-legged woman). Go another 300m (985ft) and enjoy the **Variety Kids Water Park**.

Continue along the park's seawall. You'll wind beneath the **Lions Gate Bridge**. When the bridge was constructed in 1935, local people feared that it would ruin the serenity of the park but, fortunately, their fears were unfounded. Stop just past the bridge and study the rock face for a rare, close-up 'birding' experience: cormorants, great ancient fishers that are normally very private, are nesting in the crevices. Here too was the 1888 wreck of the first steamship to sail the Pacific Coast, the Hudson's Bay paddle-wheel trading vessel *SS Beaver*, the replica of which sails the harbour for dinner cruises, tel: 682 7284.

Seawall society

Note the tide – if it's ebbing or flooding the current should be obvious – because that's what stopped the siting of one of the earliest sawmills here and helped save the land for a park.

Around **Siwash Rock** (6km/4 miles) which, according to legend, is a young native man turned to stone, English Bay opens up with Vancouver Island hazy in the distance. It's at about this point that you can't believe you're in a city, until a couple of lycraed women in their 60s jog by.

Poles in the park

But hold on: just past the next jut of land, Ferguson Point, take the steps that hook back up to the lawn and cross it for lunch at **The Teahouse Restaurant**, 2099 Beach Avenue, tel: 669 3281. This is a restaurant to treasure. The park setting, view and ambiance (complete with natural light, old wood and white linen) heighten your appetite for a great contemporary menu in one of the heritage buildings built in the days when the park was a military reserve. Choose either of the two delightful atriums rather than eating outside if you want to enjoy the view.

From the terrace of The Teahouse Restaurant you can call a cab. Or if you'd enjoy a cool forest walk, skirt around the restaurant to your left, enter the woods, then take the trail that parallels the road for 100m (300ft) intersecting Lees trail. Go left following the Bridge Road signs to a 'T', then go right, emerging at **Lost Lagoon**. Circle it and you're at the bus station, where you can ride or walk back up Robson Street to the Square.

If you're enjoying the sea walk, return to the seawall and continue past the West End high rises. The ivy-covered building is the cherished, inexpensive and usually fully booked **Sylvia Hotel**, 1154 Gilford Street, tel: 681 9321. Go one block further on and turn on **Denman Street**, one of the most entertaining streets of the city. On your left is the **Raincity Grill**, 1193 Denman Street, tel: 685 7337, $$, which serves contemporary West Coast cuisine. Across the street are various places to sit and sip a latté, eat take-away sushi, munch pizza by the slice and watch people pass by in all their permutations. And a block north is the cap on the day: **Delilah's**, 1789 Comox Street, tel: 687 3424, $$. Walk right in and put your name on the list, then kill some time by exploring the neighbourhood or sampling the famous martinis in the bar to give yourself an appetite.

I like Delilah's: because they don't take reservations, the clientele is more spontaneous, the dress is casual to elegant, the atmosphere is busy and intimate (a rare combination) and the menu is both comfortable and daring. Grilled halibut with cherries and vermouth and the Szechuan-style rack of lamb are two favourites. Please have fun. On your return up Robson Street, enjoy watching strolling couples, tourists from around the world and cars crawling at a see-and-be-seen pace. Stop in at a late-night coffeehouse and do some shopping in one of the best night-time street scenes of the city.

Girl in a Wetsuit

DAY 3

The West Side: Granville Island to Point Grey

The West Side is a day in the neighbourhoods highlighted by some of the best attractions in the region – the UBC Museum of Anthropology and the Granville Island Market – capped by a dizzying choice of Vancouver's newest cuisines.

–To starting point: from downtown Robson Square plan on walking or taking a bus to Granville Island Market. Make reservations at Bishops, tel: 738 2025. Plan for a $15 cab back to town–

The feel of quiet, cool, tree-lined streets, the lovingly lived-in Craftsmen bungalows, and the memories made in the corner bistros are what visitors to the West Side experience. It is Vancouver's experiment in living, its best views, best beaches and widest range of good, friendly, neighbourhoods all strung along Broadway Street and Fourth Avenue.

Welcome to Granville

Granville Island is a taste of Vancouver's rapid evolution from a frontier town to a city on a world scale. Once the site of numerous sawmills and heavy industry, this 15-ha (38-acre) island is a shrewd, successful and fun collection of farmers' markets, restaurants, artists' studios and water-related businesses. Granville is situated between the Burrard and Granville street bridges on the south shore of **False Creek**, a saltwater inlet that separates the West End and downtown from the Fairview and Kitsilano neighbourhoods of the West Side.

The 1.5-km (1 mile) walk from the hotel district is my personal choice. (If you choose the bus take the **No 50 False Creek South** on Granville Street and get off at Granville Island.) From any of the hotels west of Granville, go south through the well-manicured, high-rise neighbourhood to Pacific Street, which leads left into Beach Avenue. Beneath the Granville and Burrard bridges are small passenger ferries that will take you across False Creek. (Ferries run daily every 15 minutes from 7.30am–10pm. Your destination is Granville Island.)

If you've not yet had breakfast, head straight for **Isadora's** (1540 Old Bridge Street, off Duranleau Street on the southern edge of the island, just east of the vehicle causeway, tel: 681 8816 $). This

Food for thought

is one of the restaurants Vancouver does best: airy, healthy, casual and talkative. Try the whole-wheat blueberry pancakes. If you are on a late start, tour the markets first and come here for lunch. I liked the great attention to and experimentation with salads – the rainforest seasonal local greens include lovage, rocket and corn salad.

Along Granville Island's western shore **farmers' markets** are similar to London's old Covent Garden and Kuala Lampur's central market, with a shed-roofed *casbah* of vegetable stands and fruit stalls, take-out booths, fish markets and even a soup stock store. (Local cherries are sometimes heaped on tables; customers picking through them and tasting them.) From the market turn left and get a map at the **Information Centre** across the street. Reverse your course past the street entertainment plaza (always good, normally bizarre musicians, jugglers and dancers) and work around the island in a counter-clockwise direction. There are maritime businesses on your right including a boat yard, **Ecomarine Ocean Kayak Centre**, 1668 Duranleau Street, offering sea kayak retail and on-the-spot rental (*see the Itinerary Kayaking in False Creek and English Bay*).

On the east side of Duranleau Street the core buildings house the studios of well-known artisans: the late **Bill Reid**, famous for his native carving, **Gorgon Payne**, artist, and **Matt Kallio**, known for his beautiful cedar chests. They all share neighbouring storefronts around 1659 Duranleau Street. Continue down Duranleau as it bends beneath the bridge. If you're with kids, the **Kids Only Market** is what's new in toys, and just past Isadora's is **Sutcliffe Park**, a water park and playground. (Yes, your child will be soaked in two minutes.) Duranleau Street becomes Cartwright Street where the **Gallery of BC Ceramics** signals a knot of craft, glass and fabric galleries inside the circle and the **Emily Carr College of**

Anyone for a shower?

Art and Design, 1399 Johnston Street, on the waterside. You're welcome to come in and get a taste of the young art students' world and review their work, or visit the **Charles H Scott Gallery** for international exhibitions.

Just before noon, walk along Anderson Street to leave the island. At the end of the causeway (beneath the Granville Street Bridge; note the 'Island Park Walk' sign on the south side of a pylon) walk right (west) along the seawall through the new Fairview neighbourhood, with False Creek's commercial fishing boats and yachts on the right. Keep to the walk's water side to avoid the roller bladers and bicyclists. In 10 minutes you'll pass beneath the Burrard Street Bridge and spot the **Vanier Park Museum Complex** across a broad lawn. Now you have some options. There are three museums from which to pick. Check both the travelling and permanent exhibits in the complex and decide which interests you, or continue your walk westward along the shore. Either way, plan to be back on the seawall by 1–1.30pm.

Vanier Park Museum

The **Vancouver Museum** and the **H R MacMillan Planetarium** and **Pacific Space Centre** share the same conical roofed building (entrance away from the water). The Vancouver Museum, 1100 Chestnut Street, tel: 736 4431 (summer daily 10am–9pm, winter 10am–5pm, closed Monday, entry charge) gives a look at the history of the city beginning with the 8,000-year habitation of this region.

The Planetarium, tel: 738 7827 (daily in summer, closed Monday in winter) hosts a series of one-hour shows that run throughout the day and evening, featuring a 360-degree screen look at the stars in the Vancouver sky, plus travelling venues such as the *Mars Show* and the *Laser U2* programme for the rockers. Call for show times.

The **Vancouver Maritime Museum**, 1905 Ogden Avenue, at the foot of Cypress Street, tel: 257 8300 (summer daily 10am–5pm, closed Monday in winter, entry charge) lies a bit west along the shoreline trail. Regain the seawall path and go left (west) to the distinctive A-frame building sheltering the *St Roch*, the first ship to navigate the Northwest Passage from west to east and to circumnavigate North America. You get to climb aboard the actual ship and walk through the world of arctic explorers – complete with a very large stuffed walrus.

Return to the seawall west of the museum and walk **Kitsilano Beach**. On any day this is the finest spot in the urban universe – salt water, a wide sky, beach and mountains all at once. The ships anchored offshore in **English Bay** are awaiting berths to load grain, one of Canada's main exports. Across the water is the entrance to Burrard Inlet, West Vancouver, Howe Sound and off to the west, the Sunshine Coast. When the promenade turns toward the neighbourhood, just before the 100-meter, public, saltwater pool, cross busy Cornwall Street. If you are fond of Japanese cuisine for lunch, try **Kibune Sushi**, at 1508 Yew Street, tel: 731-4482.

Sophie's cosmic collection

Continue walking up Yew Street to Fourth Avenue where there are three more restaurants to choose from and which will get you to the bus as well. **Bishop's**, 2183 West Fourth Avenue, tel: 738 2025, casual-dressy, $$$, may be the favourite contemporary restaurant in the city, and the one I suggest you book for this evening's meal. **Sophie's Cosmic Café**, 2095 West Fourth Avenue, tel: 732 6810, $, is the eclectic greasy spoon and my choice for today's lunch. **Romios**, 2272 West Fourth Avenue, tel: 736 9442, $, is a Greek taverna with a good lamb shank.

Catch the No 4 UBC on West Fourth Avenue westbound to the University Loop for the Museum of Anthropology. Walk South along University Boulevard through the **University of British Columbia** campus. The oldest university in BC, incorporated in the first decade of the 20th century, its buildings are something of an architectual hodge podge but they are set in beautiful grounds, surrounded by trees. Take a right on West Mall Road then north on Marine Drive to the museum, roughly a kilometre.

The **UBC Museum of Anthropology**, tel: 822 3825/5087 (July to August daily 10am–5pm until 9pm on Tuesday; September to June Tuesday to Sunday 11am–5pm, entry charge) is in many ways the pride of the city. Designed by the internationally-honoured local architect

English Bay sunset

Arthur Erickson, the museum (usually known as MOA) is a severe, open, glass-walled, grey concrete space frame which encloses some of the monumental achievements of the First Nations people of British Columbia.

To get the best experience, buy a guide to the galleries, then enter the main hall. Here you will find marvelous examples of the indigenous culture which European settlers in the 19th century nearly succeeded in wiping out. There are massive house totems and burial totems and carved cedar masks as well as contemporary carvings of the Kwakwaka'wakw, Tsimshian, Haida and other native bands. A sliding storage tray museum allows you to examine a huge number of smaller artefacts from all over the world.

Lastly, a collection often overlooked in a wing of the museum to the left of the entry foyer is yet another ceramic coup for the city: the **Koerner Ceramics Gallery**. This is a treasure of late-15th to early-19th-century European tin-glazed and lead-glazed stoneware and earthenware.

Nearby is the authentically accurate **Nitobe Memorial Garden**, tel: 822 6038 (mid-March to mid-October, daily 10am–6pm, entry charge), a Japanese tea and stroll garden reflecting an idealized conception of nature. At the corner of 16th Avenue and SW Marine Drive, enjoy the 28-hectare (70-acre) **UBC Botanical Gardens**, tel: 822 4208 (daily 10am–6pm, entry charge).

Call a cab and either head for the hotel to change or go east for a stroll through the neighbourhood restaurant and shopping areas on Fourth Avenue between Balsam and Cypress streets, or on Broadway between Alma and Trafalgar streets. By bus, cross the street at MOA and board eastbound No 42 Chancellor (hourly, last bus 6.30pm). Or backtrack through campus to the bus loop, catching the more frequent eastbound No 4 Powell for Fourth Avenue or the No 10 or No 14 Hastings if you're choosing Broadway. These buses will take you back to town too, so save your transfers. See the *Eating Out* section for more restaurant suggestions. My choice is Bishops – I do hope you made reservations.

Museum of Anthropology

Neighborhood family

1. Chinatown

If there's one place in Vancouver that transports you to somewhere else – to pungent markets and the voices of the world – it has to be Chinatown. Take a bus from Robson Square and spend the morning in the vicinity's markets and shops. Visit a classical Chinese garden and sample dim sum at lunchtime.

Gumshan was the word that spread throughout the Pearl River region of Southeast China, bringing labourers and merchants to the 'Gold Mountain' of North America. They came first during the California Gold Rush of 1849 and then 10 years later to the Fraser River and the Caribou Mountain gold fields of British Columbia. The Chinese proved willing and resourceful, often the only reliable source of labour in the region. They worked the timber mills in the 1860s, they canned salmon along the Fraser, and from 1881–5 they came en masse to build the British Columbia section of the Canadian Pacific Railroad.

In Vancouver the Chinese Canadians settled just east of the Hastings Mill area, at first in shacks but by the turn of the century in a distinctive Chinese-style, brick-built business district known to them as Saltwater City and in time simply as Chinatown.

Today Chinatown is an historical, sensual and active community well worth an exploration. Mid-mornings are best, while the ancient Cantonese grandmothers are out shopping for the best fish and vegetables. From **Robson Square** take the No 10, 14, 16 or 20 northbound buses on Granville Street. As the route turns down East Hastings Street, the high-rises are replaced by a 1920s street scene of faded signs on rust-red brick, overhead wiring and men of another era. Leave the bus at Main Street, turn the corner going south and walk one block to East Pender Street past the copper-topped **Carnegie Centre** (built in 1902–3). Note the curious werewolf-like grotesques beneath the roof line.

Asian warmth

A tempting sign

The street signs are now bilingual and the shop window writing is in Cantonese. At Pender Street turn right and follow the left-hand sidewalk west.

The architecture now changes to narrow three-, four- and five-storey buildings with recessed balconies and touches of Chinese ornamentation. Stop in the middle of the block and look around. Although this is not the most active part of Chinatown, it is the best block both for seeing architecture and gaining a sense of the past. The upper floors of benevolent societies provided early Chinese immigrants with a respite from the racism prevalent throughout the century. And though today many of the old gaming parlours are insurance companies and accountants' offices, the second-floor restaurants still serve *dim sum* and the open-air markets spill out onto the street level.

The gaily painted Chinese gate announces the entrance to the **Chinese Cultural Centre** (ask at the centre about exhibitions) and the free opportunity to relax and stroll the **Dr Sun Yat-Sen Classical Chinese Garden**, 578 Carrall Street at Pender, tel: 689 7133. This is the first full-sized Chinese classical garden outside China. Built with traditional materials and tools, it is a re-creation of a scholars' retreat of the 14th- and 15th-century Ming period.

Horoscope stamps

Continue west, crossing Carrall Street, to the 'thinnest' building in the world, according to *Ripley's Believe It or Not*: the **Sam Kee Building**, 1.5m (not quite 5ft) wide. Cross Pender Street and return up the opposite walk to window shop in the curio stores. At the unassuming entry to **Artland**, 111 Pender Street East, order a personalized marble Chinese horoscope stamp: one end has your name carved in Cantonese, the other end has your animal sign. (The delightful woman behind the counter giggled when we discovered I was the 'Year of the Pig.')

At Main Street cross Pender Street again and, continuing up East Pender, enter the street market. You'll see hundreds of people – mostly Asian, and not only Chinese but also Vietnamese, Cambodian and Korean – all shopping. The sidewalks are narrow, the

Fresh today

grandmothers are haggling and the children are effortlessly flowing through the throng around you while the noise of humanity mingles with the scent of the true markets of the world. You might as well be in the markets of Guangzhou (Canton).

Wicker baskets, tubs and bins are filled with fresh local Yau Choy, Bau Choy (Chinese greens) and Yui Mo Qua, one of many squashes. From Thailand and Malaysia (in the summer) come the foul-smelling sweet durian and the hairy rambutangs. There are mangosteens, longan and lychee nuts. At the **Canton Enterprises** the catch is alive and includes eels, delicate blue crabs, local goeducks, gooseneck barnacles and clams (look out because they squirt). Hanging in the windows at the **Dollar Meat** shop are barbecued ducks, chickens and pork. Inside you will find trays of beef tendon and lung, chicken feet or just about any animal organ.

Continue around the corner and down Keefer Street to **Kiushun Trading Co. Ltd,** a Chinese apothecary selling ginseng, deer's horn and health herbs. Stop in **Maxim's Bakery** for an almond cookie — and note this is not a French bakery. To cap your morning in Chinatown in local style have some *dim sum*. This is a selection of meat, fish and vegetable-filled pastries, which can be very good. At 544 Main Street is the small-stair entry to **Park Lock Restaurant** where you can dine on *dim sum*, but do it before 1pm to get the best selection. To return to Robson Square go right on Main Street to the far side of East Hastings Street where you can catch any bus (except the No 16) back to Granville Street at Robson Street.

Fruit mountain

Take a morning walk along the seawall, have breakfast at Dundarave Beach, visit the old-growth coastal forest trails at Lighthouse Park and eat lunch at Horseshoe Bay.

From downtown most of the blue West Vancouver buses will take you to **Ambleside Park** (just west of the Lions Gate Bridge). Around you you'll hear snatches of French, Tamal, Portuguese, Cantonese, as strings of couples and friends deep in their common languages pass you one after the other on West Vancouver's Centennial Walk. They could be visitors, of course, but they are probably locals and they are one indication that this city is a fast-rising international star.

As you continue your walk, the cosmopolitan air of this neighbourhood will take a few more twists. Visually, it seems part Miami with its string of shoreside high-rise condos, and, farther on, part Mediterranean coast with modern villas commanding rocky sea coves. The average house price here has risen to more than $600,000, as many of the new Canadians from Hong Kong and Europe are settling higher and higher on the slopes of the North Shore mountains. They are moving here for a reason: West Van is a Big Sur neighbourhood right on the sea and deep in the forest.

Fun in the sun

Follow the relentless and seemingly ageless joggers on the continuation of Centennial Walk towards English Bay and a grand view of the bridge (built in 1938 by the Guinness family to enhance their West Van real-estate holdings). For the next 2 km (1½ miles) enjoy the shipping traffic, a few signed detours into the neighbourhood and back to the seaside and the delightful family beach at **Dundarave**, starting along the 2400 block Marine Drive.

Just up a block (crossing the tracks the **Royal Hudson Steam Train** uses en route to Squamish twice a day) is a great wall mural by Jim McKenzie of the 1792 British and Spanish meeting off Stanley Park – showing not only a land carpeted with forest but also just where the old Squamish and Musqueam villages were. Behind that wall is the best grocery store I've ever seen. At **Capers**, 2496 Marine Drive, tel: 925 3316, the owners and staff select the best and healthiest food they can find and present it in a small and comfortable space – with built-in espresso machine and a deli. Through the back of the store and up the stairs is a fine, casual and healthy café with a deck that catches the sun. This is breakfast or lunch, depending on your watch.

Lighthouse Park

For a walk in a coastal old-growth forest, and one of my favourite parks in Vancouver, cross Marine Drive and catch the No 250 Horseshoe Bay westbound. (The No 250 eastbound will take you home.) Through a neighbourhood of forest homes, the stop for **Lighthouse Park** will come up suddenly, so ask the driver to let you know. Walk down the suburban Beacon Lane and into the park. Pick one of the two main trails to the lighthouse and loop back on the other for a 5-km (3-mile) forest walk.

Back on Marine Drive catch the bus again west to **Horseshoe Bay**, a beautiful harbour tucked into the place where Vancouver runs out of room and the Coast Range meets the sea. The **BC Ferry Terminal** that routes ferries to Vancouver Island's Nanaimo and the Sunshine Coast takes up much of the town's remaining space. It is touristy, but it still manages a fine waterfront park and good fish and chips at **Troll's**, 6408 Bay Street, tel: 921 7755, overlooking the park and the harbour.

Return to Vancouver via the No 257 or the No 250 bus from the ferry terminal.

3. The Morning of the Future

Have breakfast in the architecturally flamboyant Canada Place district, visit Science World, a futuristic museum, and board the SkyTrain to New Westminster Quay for a fun picnic lunch beside the river.

Vancouver's penchant for newness, imagination and ingenuity didn't begin with Expo '86. Already accustomed to remarkably adventurous and at times bizarre architecture, high-speed ferries and high-tech lifestyles, Vancouverites take for granted the fact that their city looks like the cover of *Popular Science* magazine. But the Expo '86 theme of transportation brought the city even more: a new port of entry for the ocean-liner trade, a transport hub, and a light-rail system to speed you on your morning's adventure.

Start with a walk from Robson Square north on Howe Street toward **Canada Place** and its distinctive rooftop sails for a leisurely breakfast at **Herons** in the **Waterfront Centre Hotel's** lobby, tel: 691 1991, $$$. If you see an ocean liner berthed at Canada Place, the one-time Canada Pavilion at Expo '86 (*see Day 1 Itinerary*), take a look at one of the most modern ships in the world, then head east to the renovated **Waterfront Station**, 601 West Cordova

Science World

Street, for the **SkyTrain**. Buy a ticket for **New Westminster**, but get off at **Science World–Main Street Station** and keep your ticket for later. Head for the silver geodesic dome, the one-time Expo Preview Centre nicknamed the 'golf ball' and now the site of **Science World**, 1455 Quebec Street, tel: 443 7440 (summer: daily 10am– 6pm; winter: Monday to Friday 10am–5pm, Saturday and Sunday 10am–6pm).

Science World is a kids' world, so if you still are one, come in to a multi-level, almost totally interactive mix of science disguised as fun — from fun-house mirrors and computers (always busy), to plasma balls, floating magnets, robotics, mind puzzles, and the music machines, which are my personal favourite. If you're traveling with kids expect to spend two hours there, all adult groups probably one hour. Back on the eastbound SkyTrain enjoy the suburbs with a view of the Fraser River en route to **New Westminster Quay**.

The first major project to bring sophisticated places to the river's edge, the quay is patterned after Granville Island. The entire upper levels of the market are given over to shopping and deck restaurants, while the main floor is a true market with a mix of takeaways as well. Plan to picnic along the river wall where **The Fraser River Connection**, 800 Quayside, tel: 609 4065, a paddle-wheel riverboat, picks up passengers for a tour of **Fort Langley**. This is the birthplace of the province of British Columbia, now a restored fur-trading fort. Take the SkyTrain back at your leisure towards Waterfront Station.

New Westminster Quay

The Nitobe Memorial Garden, the UBC Botanical Gardens, the VanDusen Botanical Garden and Queen Elizabeth Park are as beautiful as they are indicative of the people and the pride of the city.

Vancouverites are serious about their gardens. They expect you to see them. So, even if you've never toured a garden before, you're going to enjoy touring them now. Four gardens stand out, ranging from the formal to the natural, from tiny to more than 40ha (99 acres) in size, and all are located on the West Side. A car will best serve this itinerary, though buses (Transit Information line: tel: 261 5100) will get you to each and every one. Make dinner reservations at **Seasons in the Park** restaurant, tel: 874 8008.

Gardener's delight

The **Nitobe Memorial Garden** , tel: 822 6038 (mid March to mid October, daily 10am–6pm), is a quiet place to begin. A formal Japanese garden, it is just 100m (330ft) up Marine Drive from the UBC Museum of Anthropology. (From downtown take either bridge south then west on Fourth Avenue, which becomes Chancellor Boulevard, then SW Marine Drive. Parking at the museum is metered and monitored.) A memorial to Inazo Nitobe, Japan's noted educator on East-West détente, the garden is a carefully tended forest walk circling a carp-filled lake and pond.

Shaded in a grove of tall firs is a large and graceful stone *Kashuga*-style lantern, one of many on the paths signifying the origins of the Japanese people. Some of these lanterns are female, others are male – for Adam and Eve – with unexpected similarities to the myths at the neighbouring Museum of Anthropology. Ask the gatekeeper for more information.

Squashes, marigolds, chocolate cosmos, Aunt Molly's ground cherries in raised beds, this is a vegetable garden to die for. Called simply 'Food Garden', it is just one of 10 unique gardens in the sprawling 47-ha (116-acre) **UBC Botanical Gardens**, tel: 822 4208. In this forest and meadow enclave there's a medicinal (*physick*) garden, a garden of therapeutic plants giving not only their Latin and common names but also the uses for each plant.

A native plant garden represents all of British Columbia – from the prickly pear cactus of the Gulf Islands to the alpine flowers of the Stikine Mountains – and there's even a winter garden that spurs Vancouver's gallant year-round gardeners with new hardy varieties of roses, irises and pansies. The gardens are all connected by a series of paths and trails that draw you to the variety and beauty of the flora; more than 400 species of rhododendrons bloom in the Asian garden alone.

The **VanDusen Botanical Garden**, tel: 266 7194, is located in the Shaugnessy neighbourhood. (Drive east on SW Marine Drive to the 'Y' taking West 41st Avenue to Oak Street. Take a left and left again on West 37th to park.) The garden hosts 22ha (54 acres) of flora from around the world. In this ambling country garden of lakes and streams, random sculpture and sculpted beds, you can almost sense the garden's previous use – as the fairways of the old Shaugnessy Golf Course. Here is the largest late-spring collection of rhododendrons in Canada, a well-tended rose garden in summer, a fragrance garden and even a corner that is going to seed – turning rural in a controlled manner – best in mid- to late-summer. **Sprinklers**, tel: 261 0011, located at the garden's main entrance, $$, is a glassed garden veranda open year-round and a fine place for a meal if you missed lunch, or if the sight of so many vegetables has given you an appetite. If so, you could eat first and then walk through the garden.

Queen Elizabeth Park is less than a mile east. (Go east on West 37th Avenue to Cambie Street; go left then right on West 33rd Avenue.) Once an old quarry and – at 150m (492ft) – still the highest point within city limits, Queen Elizabeth Park is both the city's formal garden and one of the best views around. All 50ha (120 acres) are beautifully manicured. Trails weave through the old quarries past 15-m (50-ft) waterfalls and grottoes filled with blooms. Roses, azaleas, and rhododendrons often provide the backdrop for the popular Asian wedding photo sessions.

From the other side of the hill (the park was once known as 'Little Mountain') comes the sound of baseball from the **Vancouver Angels** at the **Nat Bailey Stadium** – considered one of the great options for those with a less-than-green thumb. At the top of the hill is the **Bloedel Floral Conservatory**, tel: 257 8570, an equatorial jungle of exotic plants and free-flying tropical birds all under a great sky-lit dome. Be prepared for humidity and a small fee.

When it's near sunset, stop at Seasons in the Park restaurant, tel: 874 8008, $$$, either for a drink or for the dinner which you reserved earlier, and to admire the view of Vancouver. To return to downtown take Cambie Street north into town.

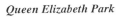

Queen Elizabeth Park

5. Vancouver's Beaches

Whether you stroll or sunbathe, swim or people-watch, you'll find Vancouver's in-city beaches exceptional. Enjoy both sides of English Bay, the grand vistas of Spanish Banks and the eccentricity of the swimming suit-optional Wreck Beach.

Vancouver – the beach? Despite a latitude about the same as London's, this is a city of delightful sandy beaches – ten, in fact – stretching for miles from Stanley Park out and around Point Grey. And in the summer you can swim; but for most people a few frantic strokes is enough, as the water temperature rarely exceeds 18°C (65°F). So grab the beach mats or walking shoes, depending on your preference and the weather.

The closest beach within walking distance of the hotel district is **Sunset** or **First Beach** on Pacific Avenue, fronting English Bay between Gilford and Nicola. **Second Beach** is just inside Stanley Park and is family oriented with a great outdoor wading pool. **Third Beach** is one of the prettiest and most secluded along the south shore of the Stanley Park seawall. These beaches are quick to get to, but my favourite beaches are further along, across False Creek on the West Side.

If you have no transportation, take the Aquabus (which runs every 15 minutes) from the east end of Sunset Beach to the Maritime Museum landing, then walk west along a shoreside promenade to **Kitsilano Beach**. This is a broad, sandy beach angled into the afternoon sun, the pride of the neighbourhood, with a generous park leading off to the residences and a string of good take-outs on Cornwall Street between Laburnum and Cypress streets: the **Flying Wedge** (pizza), **Frogurt's** (yogurt), and across Cypress is **Siegel's** (deli/bagels). On the beach there are concessions and changing rooms (as there are at most of the city beaches) and a quite

Spanish Banks skyline

Cooling off

remarkable 100-m (327-ft) outdoor saltwater pool — one of 17 public pools in the city. Visit also **Kitsilano Pool** at the north foot of Yew Street, tel: 731 0011.

Jericho, Locarno, and **Spanish Banks** are all one great strand with two long, sandy northwest-facing beaches. Beyond the beach grassy fields stretch for a mile, filled with weekend volleyball parties. Walk west from Kitsilano Beach along Point Grey Road about one kilometre to Jericho. With 45ha (111 acres) of upland lawn and mature maples meeting English Bay, Locarno is a favourite picnic beach and the site of the Vancouver international youth hostel (tel: 224 3208).

From Spanish Banks, named for the 1792 meeting between the Spanish explorers Galiano and Valdés and Captain George Vancouver, the view back to the city, mountains and sky takes your breath away. Consider running the trail that separates the beach from the lawns — it is one of the best jogs in North America.

Lastly, go to Vancouver's most loved, eccentric, and vilified **Wreck Beach**. It is a return to the 1960s as well as an education in tourism. Come prepared to take some clothes off and enjoy the community spirit of the scene. This is a clothing-optional beach grudgingly acknowledged by the city, though it has been a place for well-tanned free spirits since the 1920s. Up to 12,000 people sun themselves here on a hot weekend.

Angled right into the midday summer sun at the very end of Point Grey, Wreck Beach is 6.5sq km (2½sq miles) of great fun. You can take a 237-stair trail down through the bluff forest, pick a suitable log to lean against and pull out William Burroughs. Vendors, ethical but not quite legal, will sell you Caesar salads and whole pink grapefruits injected with 151-proof Jamaican rum.

As you might suspect, Wreck Beach is not on the map. Located below NW Marine Drive west of the Museum of Anthropology, look for the massive collection of mountain bikes. (By bus: from town take No 4 or 10 to the University Loop and walk west through campus, or from the Locarno beach hostel take the No 42.) Parking is tough. Don't take pictures unless requested, and remember to take sun screen this time.

Sunset over the sea

Ready for action

6. Kayaking in False Creek and English Bay

In the heart of the city, on Granville Island, check out the new sport of sea kayaking as a way to explore the skyline along the shores of False Creek and English Bay. Take a short walk or bus ride from Robson Square to Granville Island (*see Day 3 Itinerary*) with a windbreaker, sunglasses and sun screen. Don't even consider it unless you are a strong swimmer and have had some kayaking experience.

Sea kayaking English Bay and False Creek might be the most fun Vancouver has to offer. Pick a nice afternoon and take a reliable friend. At **Ecomarine Ocean Kayak Centre**, tel: 689 7575, on Granville Island just west of the main market off Duranleau Street, you'll be instructed, outfitted and launched. They'll go over the kayak and equipment, then give you a quick lesson on paddling, getting in and out, basic rescue, and where to go – all in about 10 minutes. For two hours paddling a single kayak rents for around $17, a double for around $27 (prices include safety equipment).

On the water, paddle slowly out through the piers of fishing boats and yachts, keeping to the right. Off Granville Island you enter False Creek – it's a busy channel, so be careful – filled with racing dragon boats, sloops and power boats, and the aquabuses shuttling to and fro. Steer right along Granville's shore beneath the Granville Street Bridge. To your right is **Sea Village**, one of the few houseboat communities in the city. Past that the 1970s condos of the Fairview Slopes march up the hill toward the **City Hall** and **Vancouver General Hospital**. At the eastern end of False Creek you will see the stainless steel 'golf ball', a remnant of Expo '86, now the **Science World** 'hands-on museum' (*see the Morning of the Future Itinerary*).

Turning back along the north shore, you will see the new construction that signals the increased influence and power of Vancouver's new Hong Kong community. New high-rise housing and offices are going up, with a generous set of urban amenities, including parks and a bike way that runs from Stanley Park all the way around False Creek to the Point Grey beaches. Cross under the bridges and paddle out into English Bay. Check the weather – it's windier out here – and check your rental time, too.

English Bay was where Vancouver's ships anchored to chart Burrard Inlet and False Creek. Follow the beaches on your right and come ashore for a stretch, if the weather permits. This is First Beach – not quite in Stanley Park and more of a neighbourhood beach for the West End apartment dwellers.

Back in your kayak head across the mouth of the bay to the Kitsilano side and the moored historical ships at the foot of the tall A-framed Maritime Museum. Old tugboats, schooners, the 'Black Duck' RCAF rescue vessel, and various classic boats (some you can visit) are all on display. Turn east and paddle beneath the Burrard Street Bridge. It was here on the southern shore that the Squamish Indian village of Snauq (meaning 'inside, at the head') was nestled up against the forest. At **Bridges** (you'll see the sign) turn in and return your kayak. Then head for the deck at **Bridges Pub**, 1551 Johnston Street, tel: 687 7351, for a Granville Island Pale Ale.

7. The North Shore

Take the SeaBus ferry to the North Shore for views of the city and the working harbour. Explore the Lonsdale Quay, have lunch, then suspend yourself on the Capilano Suspension Bridge and ride the gondola at Grouse Mountain for the best upland views of the city.

Meet the **SeaBus** at the foot of Seymour Street in the **Waterfront Station**, 601 West Cordova Street, adjacent to the Pan Pacific Centre for an 8-minute ride across Burrard Inlet. The landing is a connection for buses to 'North Van' and 'West Van,' the bedroom Vancouver communities steadily encroaching on the forest. But before you hop on a bus to the edge of the woods, check the schedule and then take some time to explore the **Lonsdale Quay Market**, 123 Carrie Cates Court, tel: 985 21 91, a busy, colourful mix of vegetable stands, fresh-fish sellers and take-away stalls, atriumed and tiered, and bustling with clothing, curio and toy shops, right on the waterfront.

Lonsdale Quay Market

It is a rare city that integrates its working harbour with any kind of public access. The quay does this with a broad, open-piered square. The SeaBus terminal flanks it on the right and the **Deas Towboat** company piers are hard on the left. Have lunch and watch the staunch little harbour tugs come and go on their ship assists and barge jobs while mammoth grain ships and container freighters glide past you toward their berths. Because nearly 10,000 local and foreign ships arrive here every year, you can expect to see more than 25 ships a day transiting the harbour.

Harbour tugs

Beyond the market at the foot of Lonsdale Avenue is a fine, southern Italian lunch and dinner restaurant known throughout Vancouver: **Corsi Trattoria**, 1 Lonsdale Avenue, tel: 987 9910, lunch Monday to Friday, dinner every night, $$. You could have a late lunch here, or book for dinner. Up Lonsdale Avenue and right on First Avenue you might wander through the nearby flea market for the oddities within, not to mention odd folk as well. But I'm not going to send you into the downtown of North Vancouver. Instead we're going to return to the SeaBus terminal for the next stop at the forest primeval.

The Grouse Mountain bus No 236 leaves through the residential district of North Vancouver that was once covered in the perpetual shade of up to 100-m (330-ft) tall fir, hemlock, and cedar trees. The massive trees fed the numerous mills that rimmed Burrard Inlet and False Creek, until the suburbs were invented. But where the Capilano River cuts deep near steep canyons en route to Burrard Inlet, many of the harder-to-get-to trees escaped the fate of their flatland brethren.

The **Capilano Suspension Bridge**, 3735 Capilano Road, tel: 985 7474, was one of the earliest of Vancouver's tourist attractions. The bridge is 140m (450ft) of undulating steel cable and plank over a 70-m (230-ft) drop to the Capilano River. It's worth it not only

Dwarfed by trees

Don't lean over

for the vertigo but also to observe the variety of human reactions it causes. The first totem poles you see were carved in the 1930s by two Danish immigrants; others by local Native Americans.

Just 200m (655ft) up the highway is **Capilano River Regional Park**, perhaps the finest forest in the city, with paths trailing along the steeply flowing river. (Listen for the continuous trill of the winter wrens and chickadees, and occasional robins.) If you're walking, take care at the narrow road entry to the park, and in about 200m (220yds) take the signed 'pipeline' trail into the **Capilano Salmon Hatchery** for a look at salmon rearing. This is also a jump-off to **Capilano Lake** and the trails looping back to the bridge. Get a trail map. If you're driving, there's ample parking at the hatchery.

Back on the Nancy Green Way (named for Canada's first Olympic gold medalist in skiing) check the sky. If it's clear, continue up hill on the Grouse Mountain bus for 10 minutes to **Grouse Mountain** and its 100-passenger aerial tram **Skyride**, tel: 986 9311. As you're whisked to 1,130m (3,700ft), prepare for a most amazing view (and in the winter, alpine skiing). Way below Vancouver looks a toy, and beyond the city sweeps a panorama of Vancouver Island and the Olympic Mountains.

If you look through the firs from the deck of the **Grouse Nest Restaurant**, tel: 984 0661, $$, (come with complimentary Skyride fares — it's a lot of money otherwise) even Mount Rainier 230km (140 miles) due south can be seen. Another way to see the view is to hike it in good tennis shoes or hiking boots. The trail begins just to the right of the parking lot entry and ascends about 2km (1½ miles) seemingly straight up through the forest. Called the **Grouse Grind**, it's a grueling scramble with scary spots and many rocks. Then return to Vancouver on the tram. Note that after 6.30pm the transit runs back to the SeaBus terminal every hour.

EXCURSIONS

Victoria is an island city, a romantic, quaint and historic seaport. As your floatplane glides toward the inner harbour, yachts pass beneath, readying for sea, and the grand Parliament buildings vie with the imposing Empress Hotel for your attention. You step ashore to the fragrance of roses mingled with salt sea air, to a festive mood and an air of unhurried ease. This excursion takes you to the Maritime Museum, Victoria's Chinatown, the Royal British Columbia Museum, and also offers a wonderful choice of restaurants for dinner.

—To the starting point: this excursion does not require a car. Plan for the day, overnight, or two nights (my preference). Reserve seats on the harbour-to-harbour Harbourair Seaplanes, tel: 688 1277 or (800) 665 0212, $$, 35 minutes, or Helijet Airways, tel: 273 1414 or (800) 665 4354, $$$, 35 minutes. By bus via the BC Ferries to the Empress take Pacific Coach Lines, tel: 662 7575, $, 3½ hours. The Canadian Pacific's Empress Hotel, tel: (800) 441 1414, $$$, is the place to stay. Reserve rooms for one or two nights and a table at the Empress Dining Room, or try the delightful Sooke Harbour House, tel: 642 3421—

Parliament Building

Victoria is a city that once dominated the frontier of British Columbia. Settled in 1843 by the Hudson's Bay Company, the choice for the site was a political one – to secure England's border with the United States. Little thought was given to its island isolation as everyone then traveled by ship – and the Hudson's Bay Company was never one to encourage settlers to interrupt its valuable fur trade. When gold was discovered in the British Columbia interior in 1858, Victoria flourished. But in the 1890s, at the height of its Victorian era, Vancouver's transcontinental railroads and ports lured away its business and its growing populace. The capital city slowed its pace, tending its gardens and its fading glory for a long, quiet century.

Victorians are very good gardeners, however, and they have nurtured their heritage well. Today Victoria is set apart from 'mere mortal cities' (as one local tour-bus driver remarked) by its colonial character and its location on the very southern tip of Vancouver Island. The waters that had separated Victoria from the headlong growth of Vancouver and Seattle – the Georgia Strait and the Straits of Juan de Fuca – now insulate this city from her neighbours' commercial hustle, making it a wonderful place to live and an unusually seductive experience for any visitor.

The beauty of a Victoria weekend begins with the ease of getting there. I recommend taking the **Harbourair Seaplanes**, tel: 688 1277, Dehavill and twin turbo Otter floatplanes adjacent to Canada Place. **Helijet**, a more expensive and equally fast helicopter flight, boards just east of the old Canadian Pacific Railway Station. Book a mid-morning flight and ask for port-side (left) seats. Leaving Vancouver's harbour, note you're flying in one of Canada's best inventions, a plane evolved from the hardy bush planes (the Otters and Beavers that still serve the remote regions of the Northern Territories). As the plane gains altitude the pilot will usually fly right over the Lions Gate Bridge and English Bay and then set a course across the usually calm, protected waters of the Georgia Strait. Weaving through the Gulf Islands, watch for pods of Orcas while traveling through some of the best maritime scenery in the world. Below you is the gulf and the US San Juan Islands, then the broad expanse of the Strait of Juan de Fuca. You may be able to see in the distance the Olympic Mountains, which mark Washington State's great Olympic Peninsula. In 30 minutes the plane banks, lands and docks right against Victoria's inner harbour seawall.

Not many cities centre on a hotel, but Victoria does. The distinctive chateau-style roof of the **Empress Hotel** commands the skyline. Ivy covers the stone and brick walls. The afternoon light filtering through the lounge catches the mahogany, rattan, crystal and

Empress Hotel

Tea lobby

silver of this 1904 National Heritage building. Though the Canadian Pacific Hotels and Resorts recently spent $45 million on renovating the 408-room Empress, they still allow the main hall's rift-cut white-oak, walnut and Brazilian red-bean wood floors to creak ever so slightly.

The Empress, named for Queen Victoria, the 'Empress of India,' is famous for its afternoon tea in the **Tea Lobby**. Reservations are a must for this traditional meal of scrumptious classic fruit preserves, Devon cream, scones, sandwiches and, of course, tea. But my friends claim the real find in the hotel is the civilized (coat and tie required) **Empress Dining Room**, considered by other restaurateurs in the area to be the measure of hotel dining in Victoria.

But Victoria is far more than the Empress. Think of this grand matron of hotels as our starting point and rest stop. Whether you are a hotel guest or just a visitor, you're welcome to explore. Take the complimentary 10.30am tour of the hotel, offered with flair and substance by the Victoria Heritage Society.

Despite Victoria's obvious tourist emphasis, there's more than enough of real interest. Let's assume it's morning and the sun is shining through the casement windows of the hotel's **Bengal Lounge**. With a good cup of Earl Grey in hand (beneath the great room's last remaining Bengal tiger skin), read the list of what you can do either within blocks of the hotel or further afield.

Victoria – like Vancouver – is compact, only more so. Walking is easy: the harbour, fine neighbourhoods, historical and shopping districts and waterfront parks are all close. And the weather is sunnier here than in Vancouver; much drier with nearly a third less rain: 619mm (24in) to Vancouver's 1,588mm (62in) annually.

Leaving the hotel note the **Gray Line Tours** (tel: 388 5248) bright red, English-built, double-decker buses out front. This 1½-hour narrated tour through both the city and the neighbourhoods is fine if you want to see a lot of sights quickly (it runs every half hour). But it is not an on-and-off option and the buses tend to be rather cramped, so avoid it on a hot day.

On foot is best. First, loop through town by taking **Government Street** which fronts the hotel, then, crossing at Wharf

Young entrepreneurs

Government Street banner

Street, stop in the art deco **Travel Information Centre** for a map. Then follow the shoreline to visit the moored yachts, noting the ocean-going sailing vessels with their self-steering rigs. This is the port of many a transpacific yacht as well as the biannual **Victoria-Maui Race.** Several **whale-watching** excursions depart from the dock in front of the Empress Hotel. At 1107 Wharf Street the **Emily Carr Gallery** exhibits work by artists of Carr's era. At Bastion Square the **Maritime Museum of BC**, tel: 385 4222 (daily 9.30am–4.30pm), not only has 5,000 nautical artifacts but also the best nautical bookstore on the island. Go north (left) on Government Street, passing Victoria's **Chinatown** with its beautiful **Gates of Harmonious Interest**. Chinatown was once a district with many gambling houses and legal opium factories. Today shops sell Asian goods along **Fan Tan Alley,** the narrowest street in Canada.

One block farther north on Herald Street my choice for lunch is the **Herald Street Caffe**, 546 Herald Street, tel: 381 2218 (Wednesday to Sunday brunch). In a town with a lot of tourism there are a surprising number of good stores. Returning on the waterside of Government Street, stop in at **Munro's Books**, 1108 Government, one of Canada's finest bookstores. Cross the street for chocolates at the legendary **Rogers' Chocolates** and you're back at the hotel.

Here are three more suggestions before you rest. The **Royal British Columbia Museum**, 675 Belleville Street, tel: 387 3014 (daily 10am–5.30pm), is the attic of the province and the location of the **National Geographic Theatre**. The museum contains groves

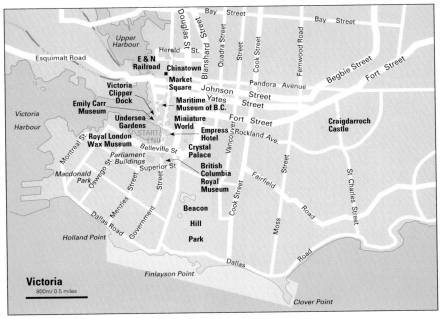

53

of priceless totem poles, George Vancouver's great ship's cabin as it was in 1792, a Kwa-gulth winter longhouse, an uncannily lifelike forest to walk through, as well as a turn-of-the-century town, innovative films and a full-sized mammoth. Everyone loves this museum. Start by renting the taped tour — yes, it really is good — and plan for two hours of intravenous knowledge. As an add-on you can visit several **Heritage Houses**, tel: 387 4697, fully-restored and furnished period houses throughout the city. They are open daily throughout the summer. Check in advance on winter opening hours.

To reach **The Butchart Gardens**, tel: 652 5256 (daily 9am–sunset, entry charge) by bus, connect at 75 Central Saanich. Call Victoria Transit: 382 6161 ($2) for stops and times. Euphoric gardeners love this formal garden, a former quarry taken over by the ambitious Jenny Butchart when her cement-making husband ran out of limestone. From 1904 to the present the garden has grown to 20ha (50 acres) of year-round blooms with over a million bedding plants rotated through different areas each season. The only drawbacks are the strong sense of commercialism and crowds during the high-bloom and tourist season.

Sooke Harbour House, 1528 Whiffen Spit Road, Sooke, tel: 642 3421, $$$, is the ultimate dining dream of British Columbians. Located 22km (14 miles) west of Victoria overlooking the Strait of Juan de Fuca, the Sooke Harbour House is a thoughtfully appointed lodge built around Fredrica and Sinclair Philip's sunlit restaurant which has an international reputation and is consistently voted one of the top five restaurants in Canada. Fredrica and Sinclair use the finest local fish, meat and vegetables flavoured with herbs from the gardens surrounding their house. If you can get a room ($$$), do so. It's best to arrive by cab from Victoria. This is expensive, but worth it.

Sooke Harbour hosts

Additional dining and late-night options in Victoria include: **The Garlic Rose**, 1205 Wharf Street, tel: 384 1931, $$, offering seafood platters served Mediterranean-style with a wide choice of pastas; and **Spinnaker's Brewpub**, 308 Catherine Street, tel: 386 2739, $, which has a great waterfront deck and BC micro-brewery beer – this is the local definition of a relaxing Canadian summer afternoon.

Szechuan, 853 Caledonia Avenue, tel: 384 5651, $$. Joseph Wong's restaurant is the best place in Victoria for fresh seafood. (Trucks loaded with fish arrive in the middle of the night.)

Pagliacci's, 1011 Broad Street, tel: 386 1662, $, is one of the only bohemian coffeehouses (good pizza, fair cheese cake, easy jazz) in town. **Barb's Place**, 310 Saint Lawrence Street, tel: 384 6515, $, serves fish and chips at Fisherman's Wharf Park. It's a local hangout and take away.

Pick up a copy of the free *Monday Magazine* for current information on cultural events and entertainment. On your return by plane try port side again for a good look at Victoria, Vancouver Island, the Gulf Islands and the Coast Range.

2. Gulf Islands: Galiano

'The water is cool but can be quite pleasant on an incoming tide,' reads the official guide for Galiano Island in the heart of the Gulf Islands. Rural to wild and unquestionably beautiful, quaint with a touch of British rustic, the Gulf Islands are a refuge from Vancouver's urbanity. Served by frequent ferry, this string of 11 major islands and about 200 smaller ones is popular with visitors and locals alike.

—Begin by securing overnight accommodations and dinner reservations at Galiano Island Lodge and Resort, tel: 539 3388, $$$, or by calling the Canadian Gulf Islands B&B Reservations Service, tel: 539 5390. Then secure car ferry reservations from Tsawwassen to (and from) Galiano on BC Ferries, tel: 888-223 3779. You can also fly Harbourair, tel: 688 1277. A floatplane will take you from downtown Vancouver to Galiano Lodge in 35 minutes—

Located across the Georgia Strait in the weather lee of Vancouver Island, the Gulf Islands have a Mediterranean-type climate of extended summers and dry winters – **Galiano** has an average of only 46cm (18in)

Island ferry

of rain per year – making the islands a great year-round destination. Most of them have dry woodlands, sandy beaches and rocky outcrops, and the marine life is fascinating.

Of the three central Gulf Islands, **Pender** and **Saltspring** are the most popular. Pender is known for its many beaches and delightful coves while Saltspring is the biggest and most developed and its modern seaside resort, **Ganges**, has all the usual tourist amenities. Accommodation ranges from the expensive but highly recommended Hastings House, to campsites located in the **Ruckle Provincial Park**. But although these islands have more amenities (and are also accessible via the Tsawwassen ferry), they also have more people per square kilometre. Our excursion will be to Galiano, the wilder, simpler choice.

The Tsawwassen ferry terminal is located south of Vancouver on Highway 99 (take Granville Street south and follow signs to 'Fer-

Galiano girl

ries, US Border'). Turn west on Highway 17 to Tsawwassen Terminal. Allow enough time to arrive one hour early. The direct sailing is a morning one across the shipping lanes of the Georgia Strait and through the strong currents of Active Pass to Sturdies Bay.

Driving off the ferry dock note the people: some local, some visitors. The 76-sq km (29-sq mile) island you are entering is home to no more than 800 year-round residents. Take the first left (cutting through the waiting off-island cars) to Galiano Lodge or continue to the Tourist Information Centre on the right for a map of the island, then follow the road to the fork, taking a left on Montague Harbour Road to the centre of town.

On the left is the **Corner Store** and **Ixchel Crafts**, which features women's art of the island and the Americas. On the right is the **Day Star Market** with its ever changing names. Some say, 'Just call it the **Market Café**.' Buy some picnic food for later then settle in for some tea, fresh baked goods, great salads and a closer look at the local people. There's always an issue on the island – often over the timber rights of this heavily forested land.

On the road again stay on Montague Harbour Road and follow the signs to **Montague Harbour Provincial Park** with its two beaches, where there is a chance to do some fishing or digging for clams. There are a number of campsites in the park. Information about these and about national and provincial parks in general is obtainable from tourist offices or the BC Parks office (*see Useful Addresses in the Practical Information section*). Look for evidence of an old village site along the beach because archaeological digs have unearthed ancient Coast Salish sites and vast midden deposits, evidence that the island was inhabited by the Salish Indians for thousands of years before Dioniso Galiano, a Spanish naval commander, explored the area in 1792. He bequeathed his surname to the island and his first name to the next provincial park you will come to.

Montague Harbour

At the end of the western point is a good spot to settle down for a while — remember, this is a relaxing overnight stay. Keep an eye out for kingfishers, eagles, oyster-catchers, cormorants, harbour seals and leopard slugs, too. Back on the main road take a right and head west (up island) on Portlier Pass Road for about 18km (11 miles), turn right on Cook Road and follow it to signs for **Dionisio Point Provincial Park**, one of the most beautiful park sites you'll ever see. Take your lunch and, being careful not to trample on the wild flowers (the little succulents are called stonecrop) head for the point and a sweeping view of Portlier Pass (with currents of up to 10 knots) and the northern Georgia Straits.

Once you've returned to Portlier Pass Road turn right (west) for a short stop at **Spanish Hills General Store** and an iced latté.

Go just past the **Hummingbird Pub** (a local favourite) and check the Community Hall for that evening's programme. Anything from plays to country dancing might be going on, giving you a good look at the island's gregarious side. For dinner there's competition. At **Galiano Island Lodge** Frank Leung and Lesley McKay have patterned their waterfront lodge after Sinclair and Fredrica Philip's Sooke Harbour House (*see Excursion to Victoria*), with the beginnings of a herb garden and an ambitious menu.

To find the **Woodstone Country Inn**, tel: 539 2022, take a left off Sturdies Bay Road to Georgeson Road and follow signs to yet another ambitious dining room. The fixed-price, four-course dinner uses fresh island vegetables and fruits. Both places are within walking distance and give you a great excuse to stroll back beneath the stars to your lodgings and the morning ferry.

Seafood supper

Deep into the Coast mountains, a scenic fjord drive leads to one of the best international skiing and summer sports resort towns in North America, with activities that will suit all tastes at all times of the year.

–Plan to stay one to two nights and consider the weather. The winter season is from mid-November–April. Summer is best from July–September. Make reservations through Whistler Chalets and Accommodations, tel: 683 3399, and ask for the Canadian Pacific Chateau Whistler (direct booking, tel: 938 2092), $$$, the finest of the big hotels, or the Delta Whistler Resort (direct booking, tel: 932 1982), $$, for a mid-range stay. For dinner call the Keg of the Mountain, tel: 932 5151, $$$. Alternative transportation includes BC Rail, tel: 984 5246, which has daily passenger service to and from Whistler. Maverick Coach Lines, tel: 255 1171, has six daily bus departures from the Vancouver bus depot at 1150 Station Street–

A mountain hike

Thirty years ago the Whistler Valley was a few fishing lodges and isolated homesteads; there was no town, just a highway cutting beneath the high, glaciated mountains of the Coast Range. Today Whistler is a four-season resort located just two hours away from Vancouver, featuring a myriad of hotels, luxury condominiums, pensions, hostels, restaurants, cafés and pubs, all found in an attractive and very crisp alpine village setting.

Golf courses threaten to overrun the valley. Everyone jogs, mountain bikes and skis. What has been created is not just a new town but also a new lifestyle for those who can anticipate roller blading into their senior years. Vancouver writer Steve Threndyle calls the skiing resort a 'Disneyland for Adults'. Whistler is the international new-kid-on-the-block resort, highly praised by skiiers and critics alike, and an irresistibly attractive destination for those who value great scenery, outdoor sports and rustic elegance.

Start out early and plan for a two-hour drive (two- to three-hours in winter) by crossing the Lions Gate Bridge to the North Shore, and following the signs for West Vancouver/Highway 99. Turn right on Taylor Way and then left (west) onto the four-lane Upper Levels Freeway. Approaching Horseshoe Bay, follow the signs to Squamish/Whistler. Passing Horseshoe Bay, one of the world's truly great drives begins, full of drama and wild beauty.

Named the **Sea-to-Sky Highway**, the two-lane Highway 99 climbs, dips and winds along the sheer cliffs of Howe Sound. Drive carefully and view a true fjord, representative of much of the 25,800-km (16,000-mile) coastline of British Columbia. At Brittania Beach you can visit the inner workings of an old copper mine at the **BC Mining Museum**, tel: 688 8735 (May, June and September: Wednesday to Sunday 9.30am–4pm; July–August: daily 9.30am–4pm). Or just short of Squamish, right off the road, visit **Shannon Falls**, BC's third-highest waterfall – 340m (1,111ft) high. In winter look for ice climbers here. In summer a kilometre up the highway the **Stawamus Chief**, a 650-m (2,140-ft) high granite massif attracts rock climbers.

North of Squamish, the aptly-named Diamond Head peak dominates the skyline to the east. This stark summit is the scooped-out remnant of Mount Garibaldi, an extinct volcano that forms part of the Pacific Rim ring of fire. Another volcanic remnant, the Black Tusk, is visible farther north. Both areas are located in **Garibaldi Provincial Park** and feature extensive hiking trails, well-marked by blue-and-white park signs on the roadside.

The officially-named **Resort Municipality of Whistler** is the only town in Canada which was founded as a ski resort. Although the ski area and the town share the same name, 'going to Whistler' generally refers to the entire region. **Whistler Mountain** opened in 1967 exclusively as a winter weekend getaway for Vancouverites; it evolved as a great expert/intermediate mountain with virtually no amenities. The opening of adjacent **Blackcomb Mountain** and subsequent development of the Euro-flavoured **Whistler Village** changed the valley forever and vaulted the area into destination resort super-stardom.

Famous for skiing, the two mountains – Blackcomb and Whistler

Skiing on Blackcomb

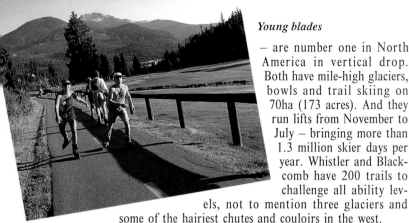

Young blades

— are number one in North America in vertical drop. Both have mile-high glaciers, bowls and trail skiing on 70ha (173 acres). And they run lifts from November to July — bringing more than 1.3 million skier days per year. Whistler and Blackcomb have 200 trails to challenge all ability levels, not to mention three glaciers and some of the hairiest chutes and couloirs in the west.

Each mountain deserves a full day. Contact the **Whistler and Blackcomb Activities and Information Centre**, tel: 932 2394.Winter or summer you can ride the gondola (or 'quad') chairs to the top. Enjoy the Coast Range view over lunch on the veranda at any of a number of side by side restaurants in tiny **Whistler Village**. Try **Ingrid's Village Café**, $, at Skiers Plaza, or my long-standing favourite Italian restaurant for both lunch and dinner, **Il Caminetto Umberto's**, tel: 932 4442, $$$.

For box lunches and no crowds try a day of helicopter skiing with **Tyax Heli-Skiing**, tel: 932 7007. (You must be a strong intermediate skier and bring around $350. Tyax will bring the chopper and the lunch.)

Surprisingly the Whistler/Blackcomb summer is its winter's equal. There's an embarrassment of outdoor activities (with guides and rentals at reasonable rates). You can play golf, roller blade, hike, swim, paraglide, river-raft, canoe, kayak, sail, windsurf, horse ride, fly-fish, rockclimb, hot-air balloon, jet-boat, play tennis, and even ski through July high up on the **Horstman Glacier** on Blackcomb Mountain. If you want to ride a mountain bike the lazy way,

Whistler snacks

reserve all the gear at **Bike Stop**, tel: 932 3659, for a guided lift up towards the top in the gondola and an exhilarating, don't-hit-your-front-brakes ride down Whistler Mountain.

All summer long there's classical and country-and-blues music festivals, summer theatre, photography workshops and even Saturday-night star gazing from the top of Blackcomb Mountain (with the Vancouver Planetarium's portable telescopes).

Back in the valley, in the village, take a stroll through the inviting streets. Many are pedestrian-only and all are filled with a variety of alluring restaurants and shops (marvel at some of the most expensive skiwear on earth). It's a short woods walk between Whistler Village and Blackcomb's newer and just-as-tastefully done village. Enjoy the heather- and hemlock-scented air while you wonder just how sore your muscles will be tomorrow.

Here's a listing of additional lodges and restaurants. European influence is found in two pensions: the **Durlacher-Hof**, tel: 932 1924, $$, and retired French Olympic ski coach Jacques Morel's **Edelweiss Pension**, tel: 932 3641, $$. Both successfully combine the log-cabin ambiance of the North American West with an old-world intimacy prevalent in the design covenants throughout the valley.

Restaurants include the architecturally delightful **Monk's Grill**, tel: 932 9677 $$, and the Chateau Whistler's **The Wildflower**, tel: 938 2033, $$, both of which are located at the base of Blackcomb. In the village you can join the Japanese camcorder crowd for sushi at the two locations of **Sushi Village**, tel: 932 3330, $.

Bikes and bunkers

There are only two Whistler area restaurants reviewed in *Where to Eat in Canada*, one of which is a cousin of Vancouver's terrific French restaurant **Le Crocodile**, so look out for **Val D'Isere**, tel: 932 4666, $$$. Another option, **Crepe-Montagne**, tel: 905 4444, $$, is best known for its no-frills breakfast (try the farmer's omelette), then at night it has a different chef and staff turning out the best dinner to be found in Whistler in this moderate price range.

Night life is a mix of live music at **The Savage Beagle Bar** and other rock'n'roll, see-and-be-seen night clubs. The **Mallard Bar** in the Chateau Whistler offers intimate piano/cabaret entertainment. And there's always the movies at the in-village **Rainbow Theatre**, tel: 932 2422.

Here's one final piece of advice: time your return trip to Vancouver to coincide with a sunset over Howe Sound.

Shopping

Vancouver is a great place for people who rarely shop. The high quality, range of tastes, strong European roots and the imaginative home-grown talent in window after shop window works. What you see is due to a strong single-owner ethic that strives for the one-of-a-kind item that you won't find in a chain retailer (this is one reason why there are not a lot of chain or franchise stores in Vancouver). Best of all a vibrant, relatively young and affluent inner-city community supports this creativity. The result is often the unique store – the one that even reluctant shoppers can't resist. Equally important is the price. Canada is keeping the dollar low compared to the rest of the Commonwealth and the United States dollar – goods cost less here (currently 15–30 percent depending on the currency), and you can turn in your GST Tax on departure (*see Practical Information*).

Vancouver has its department stores and its shopping malls but the most interesting discoveries are in the older shopping districts, where retailers tend to be both discriminating and exuberant. Over the years these districts have created shopping enclaves – neighbourhoods specializing in one type of merchandise. Here are some of the shopping high, hot and odd spots.

Robson Street, an eclectic, casual, designer-clothes dominant avenue between Hornby and Jervis, is the closest area in Vancouver to an enclave for clothing.

For men: **Emile Klein Men's Wear**, 1285 Robson Street, tel: 608 4242. For women: **Margareta Designs**, 948 Robson near Hornby, tel: 681 6612, $$–$$$: casual, high fashion, own-label designs. For men and women: **Straiths**, 900 West Georgia, tel: 685 3301, $$–$$$: located in the Hotel Vancouver, features 'contemporary fashion – Burberrys to Ungaro – from the very classic to the very fashion forward'. Ask the clerks for other store recommendations, for most of the best clothiers are spread throughout the downtown area.

Robson Street shoppers

Enticing gifts

Across False Creek, the **South Granville Street** district between West Seventh and West 15th streets has been steadily attracting new fashion retailers as well as fine arts and antique dealers. **Zonda Nellis Designs**, 2203 Granville Street, tel: 736 5668, $$$: weaves her own fabrics into lines of knitwear for women. **The Quality Custom Shirtmakers**, 1445 West Broadway, tel: 731 9190, $$, fits a custom shirt for between $38 and $90. The wait is two weeks' long and then you can order by mail. This neighbourhood has also long been an enclave for oriental rug dealers. Nearby is **Granville Island** which caters to people interested in art and crafts, house and kitchen goods. Its shopping highlights are in the Day 3 Itinerary.

Victorian street lamps line the cobblestone streets of historic **Gastown**, where Vancouver begun. Located along Water Street just one block from the cruise ship dock at **Canada Place**, boutiques, galleries and restaurants occupy restored warehouses and refurbished 19th-century alleyways. Visit here for an assortment of cigar stores, souvenirs, native Indian crafts and costume jewelry. West two blocks is the **Vancouver Pen Shop Ltd**, 512 West Hastings Street, tel: 681 1612, where you can find both antique and new pens.

This close to the wilderness, the outdoor stores are superb. The **Fairview district** just east of Granville has most of them: **Mountain Equipment Co-op**, 428 West 8th, tel: 872 7858, is the biggest and most complete. **Coast Mountain Sports**, 2201 West 4th Avenue, tel: 731 6181, is the LL Bean of Canada.

In the 1960s the **Kitsilano** neighbourhood (*see Day 3*) was the college students' mecca. Today the residents are still on the edge of the counter-culture but their houses are worth $400,000. Nonetheless the legacy is obvious in the string of health, healing, occult and natural foods stores on Broadway between Trafalgar and Alma and the speciality stores on West 4th Avenue from Burrard to Alma. The bohemian atmosphere of vegetarian and ethnic restaurants intermingles with the contemporary style of *haute cuisine* bistros and trendy coffee bars. Elegant kitchen emporiums nestle next to funky New Age crystal palaces.

'Trad' traders

Forty Winks, 1854 West 1st Avenue, carries fine European linens and white goosedown comforters. **Lucina Luna**, 1835 West 4th Avenue, offers charming candles and accessories. **Banyen Books and Sound**, a bookstore with an adjacent music store, 2671 West Broadway, tel: 732 7912, is the best place to start. To centre yourself, head for **Benny's Bagels**, 2505 West Broadway, tel: 731 9730, the 24-hour coffee house sidewalk café.

Handmade boots

Bookstores abound in Vancouver. Try **Duthie's**, 919 Robson at Hornby, tel: 684 4496. This is the best for general books. **Mystery Merchant**, 1952 West Fourth near Cypress, tel: 739 4311, sells new and used mysteries in a Victorian bookstore setting. **Sophia Bookstore**, 725 Nelson near Granville, tel: 684 4032, specializes in Asian and Japanese books and magazines. **The Travel Bug**, 2667 W Broadway, tel: 737 1122, is a fine travel bookstore, with maps and travel accessories too. **Vancouver Art Gallery Gift Shop**, 750 Hornby at Robson, tel: 682 2765, is the best in town for art and gift books. **Women In Print**, 3566 West 4th, tel: 732 4128, has lots of books for, by and about women.

World Wide Books and Maps, 736 Granville near Georgia, tel: 687 3320, is a great shop for travel books, all the BC quadrangles and city maps. **City of Vancouver Planning**, 453 West 12th Avenue, tel: 873 7344, is the place to go when you are really in need of maps and statistics.

Ten years ago **Yaletown** along Mainland Street was little more than a dilapidated cluster of old warehouses. Today the industry is gone and Yaletown addresses are the trendiest in town. Restaurants, funky pubs, artists' lofts and high fashion clothing stores entertain passers-by. Visit **A Different Place**, 1035 Mainland Street, for unusual home fashions, or **Barbara Jo's Books for Cooks**, 1128 Mainland, to fulfill your chef's dreams. **Atomic Model Boutique**, 1036 Mainland, offers brand name fashion such as Tocca, Vivienne Westwood and Anna Sui, while **Reminiscence** at 1202 Homer Street carries Chinese antique furniture, armoires, cabinets, chests and chairs. The old warehouse loading bays spill out into patio areas forming part of steak and seafood establishments.

Additional stores of practical, local and whimsical value across the city include:

Leo's Camera Supply, 1055 Granville near Nelson, tel: 685 5331. For 40 years *the* camera store in Vancouver, it's good for speciality filters, used lenses and obscure equipment too. **Hanson's Fishing Outfitters**, 102-580 Hornby Street, tel: 684 8988, specializes in salmon and fly fishing equipment. They will also give regional information and advice on the best fishing locations and tackle, boat rental and licence regulations. **Dayton Shoe Co. Ltd**, 2250 East Hastings Street, tel: 253 6671, has shoes that go beyond Doc Martens – handmade motorcycle boots, etc. The **Inuit Gallery**, 345 Water Street in Gastown, tel: 688 7323 is one of the best First Nations art galleries in North America, where friendly staff will help you understand aboriginal art. Definitely worth a browse.

Antiques galore

Eating Out

'The unrepentant exuberance of the west coast', a quote from *Where to Eat in Canada*, sums up the adventure of dining in Vancouver. With more than 2000 restaurants in competition, there are so many good restaurants chasing many great ones in this town. The energy is everywhere – in the neighbourhoods, in the ethnic business districts, the bustling downtown core, the rural inns. Even the hotels, usually bastions of the status quo, are attentive and ambitious.

What works in Vancouver? A mix of ingredients: Northwest greens, salmon, and shellfish. Influences from California, the Southwest, Europe's strength and Asia's fusion blend together to form Vancouver's enviable cuisine. BC wines have joined the award-winning ranks of the great vintners and though priced heftily are popular and enjoyable.

The list of eateries that follows is a sampler, by neighbourhood, of the range and ingenuity of the chefs and the cuisine of Vancouver. Note that prices quoted are in Canadian dollars and include a meal for one person with wine. $ = $5–$20; $$ = $20–$40; $$$ = $40 and up.

Nouveau but nice

Downtown

LE CROCODILE
909 Burrard Street, entrance on Smithe
Tel: 669 4298
There is a subdued excitement when dining in this very best of French restaurants. The French-Alsatian menu and impeccable service add up to a fine evening. $$$

CHARTWELL
The Four Seasons
791 West Georgia Street
Tel: 689 9333
From a comfortably elegant polished wood and leather setting, chef Wolfgang von Weiser produces a menu that is born in Europe, matured in Vancouver and touches the Pacific Rim for excitement. A lovely restaurant. $$$

BANDI'S
1427 Howe Street at Pacific
Tel: 685 3391
Hungarian cuisine in one of the last Swiss chalet bungalows of the Downtown area. $$

WILLIAM TELL
765 Beatty Street across from BC Place
Tel: 688 3504
The Georgian Court Hotel's venerable restaurant, with Continental cuisine of a richness and variety unsurpassed in the city. $$$

GALLERY CAFÉ
750 Hornby Street
Tel: 688 2233
Lunch in the Vancouver Art Gallery. Excellent salads and light fare. $

Chinatown

PHNOM PENH
244 East Georgia Street
Tel: 682 5777
Hot and sour prawn soups and surprising salads, simple decor, low prices, and good food. $

PARK LOCK RESTAURANT
544 Main Street
Tel: 688 1581
Dim sum is the specialty in this classic Chinatown favourite. The earlier you arrive, the better the selection. $

THE ONLY CAFÉ
20 East Hastings Street
Tel: 681 6546
The Only Café is a legendary fish and chips joint, and the oldest restaurant in Vancouver. $

FLOATA SEAFOOD RESTAURANT
400–180 Keefer Street
Tel: 602 0368
Experience the delights of *dim sum* or Cantonese cuisine. $$

The West End

DELILAH'S
1789 Comox Street
Tel: 687 3424
Delilah's mixes a contemporary west coast menu with good martinis and a

good-looking West End clientele. This is my favourite romantic restaurant. They don't take reservations, so just go, get on the list and stroll Denman Street until your table's ready. $$

CINCIN RISTORANTE
1154 Robson Street
Tel: 688 7338
You'll like CinCin for the warm terracotta and the open kitchen; you'll also like the food: the Tuscan-Mediterranean tastes of grilled red peppers, eggplant (aubergine), lamb and garlic. $$

THE BREAD GARDEN
1880 West First Avenue
Tel: 738 6684
This recommendaton is part of a chain (there are six branches) but it started here and it's the best bakery around. And it's open 24 hours. $

TRUE CONFECTIONS
866 Denman Street
Tel: 682 1292
Vancouver's best desserts, cream pies and cheese cakes. $$

CIAO BELLA
703 Denman Street
Tel: 688 5771
Authentic Italian cuisine and a romantic piano bar atmosphere prevail here. $$$

Kitsilano / Point Grey

BISHOPS
2183 West Fourth Avenue
Tel: 738 2025
'Nothing comes closer to culinary perfection than Bishops', is the singing endorsement of a local guidebook. $$$

TROPIKA
3105 West Broadway
Tel: 737 6002
Vibrant flavours of Malaysian dishes including *satay*. $$

NYALA RESTAURANT
2930 West 4th Avenue
Tel: 731 7899
Daily specials of African food and a vegetarian buffet. $$

CHIANTI CAFÉ AND RESTAURANT
1850 West Fourth Avenue
Tel: 788 8411
Chianti is a Kitsilano favourite – it has an extensive traditional menu, lots of food and a bustling atmosphere. $

2000 restaurants to choose from

AFGHAN HORSEMEN
445 West Broadway
Tel: 873 5923
Authentic Afghan cuisine from vegetarian to tender marinated shish kebabs. You can even be seated on floor cushions. $$

ALMA STREET CAFÉ
2505 Alma Street
Tel: 222 2244
An inventive vegetarian and carnivorous menu plus *good* live jazz most evenings. Draws a clientele from the University of British Columbia. $

Brunch at Capers

SOPHIE'S COSMIC CAFÉ
2095 West Fourth Avenue
Tel: 732 6810
The eclectic breakfast/lunch/dinner non-greasy spoon with the best memorabilia in the city. $

Fairview / Commercial

ISADORA'S
1540 Old Bridge Street
Granville Island
Tel: 681 8816
One of the restaurants which Vancouver does best: airy, talkative, great experimentation with salads. Try the halibut herb cakes. Great for breakfast. $

TOJO'S
202-777 West Broadway
Tel: 872 8050
Hidekazu Tojo's sushi bar is the centre of the culinary earth for many a Vancouverite. Master chef/owner Tojo-san's favourites are the Rainbow maki, Tojo's tuna, and the Golden Roll. $$$

TOMATO FRESH FOOD CAFÉ
3305 Cambie Street
Tel: 874 6020
A diner devoted to a '50s' tomato motif and light-hearted fare. $

SANTOS TAPAS
1191 Commercial Drive
Tel: 253 0444
Grilled sardines and squid, garlic potatoes and sangria. $

RUBINA TANDOORI
1962 Kingsway
Tel: 874 3621
East Indian food with spices like anaise, cardamom, clove and cinnamon that are well acquainted with chicken, beef, and lamb. Rubina Tandori is one of the best and you'll *love* the decor. $$

Frivolous fish

North Shore

CAPERS
2496 Marine Drive at 25th
West Vancouver
Tel: 925 3316
Tucked behind the best grocery store in the region is a small sunny-decked, healthy food café which serves free-range eggs and nitrate-free bacon. Expect a queue for brunch and no dinner on Sunday. $

CORSI TRATTORIA
1 Lonsdale
North Vancouver
Tel: 987 9910
A true Italian repast at the foot of Lonsdale, adjacent to the SeaBus terminal. $$

SALMON HOUSE ON THE HILL
2229 Folkestone Way
West Vancouver
Tel: 926 3212
Salmon and trout are the specialties, with an inventive *dim sum* and a view of Vancouver that is breathtaking. $$$

Nightlife

As in the densely populated continental cities, over 125,000 people live in the urban core. These are the people who set a tone, an ambiance, for the city as a whole. As a result Vancouver is truly an entertainment city with a busy and safe night-time street scene. People are out dancing at the Commodore, dining in the cafés, or just strolling along the avenues way into the wee small hours. They feed a growing counter-culture theatre community and staff the festivals that inundate Vancouver in the summer.

Culture tends to be on a fairly small scale, driven by coteries of talented artists on tight budgets. What they produce is rich and varied. They're supported to a degree by the federal government, but sadly the entire arts community is largely ignored by the business community. Until the manner of business sponsorship evolves, Vancouver's premiere venues, the symphony, opera, theatre and the rising younger artists will be continually strapped.

The most European aspect of Vancouver's entertainment is its evening walks. Denman Street in the

On the town

Movie time

West End, Robson between Jervis and Burrard, the old Greek neighbourhood in Kitsilano, the Portuguese and Italian districts around First and Commercial — these are the old streetcar neighbourhoods of Vancouver which are perfect for an evening stroll. The result is reminiscent of a summer night in the streets and squares of Milan where everyone will be out for the *giretto*, the 'stroll'. It is pleasantly crowded, with seemingly all the world's faces out for an espresso, a late supper, window shopping and flirting. This is where you'll find the heart of Vancouver. Here are four great neighbourhoods to visit one foot in front of the other:

Robson Street in the West End between Burrard and Denman is the most popular of night-time walks. At **Denman Street**, turn left and walk to the shore of English Bay. This is the ultimate in people-watching and a favourite stroll at sunset too.

West Broadway between Trafalgar and Dunbar is the best of the neighbourhood strolls. It is a loose Greek enclave between Balaclava and MacDonald that will pull you in for a glass of raki.

The Grandview District around First and Commercial contains the old Italian and Portuguese neighbourhoods — open air markets and bistros now evolving due to an influx of young moderns.

Granville Street between Robson and Drake has long been considered the entertainment district of Vancouver — the **Commodore**, the **Orpheum**, the **Vogue**, the **Paradise**, the **Granville**, the **Caprice** and the **Capitol** theatres are the legacy of the late 1920s–40s heyday of what is known as Theatre Row. Today they still open their doors to the Vancouver Symphony, show first-run movies and are used as a venue for both old and new popular music.

What's on tonight

The following is a list of particular venues to consider. For a current recording of arts and entertainment in Vancouver call the **Arts Hotline**, tel: 684-ARTS (684 2787). Tickets for most major events are through **TicketMaster**, tel: 682 1306. Lastly, the most useful guide for just about everything in Vancouver is the weekly, free *Georgia Strait* available at stores and newsstands.

71

FORD CENTRE FOR PERFORMING ARTS
777 Homer Street
Tel: 602 0616
Big name productions and musicals in a glitzy major theatre.

Comedy Clubs

TQ'S MUSICAL COMEDY RESTAURANT
6897 120th Street, Delta
Tel: 591 2229

YUK YUKS COMEDY CLUB
750 Pacific Boulevard So
Tel: 687 5233

Repertory Movie Theatres

THE HOLLYWOOD
3123 West Broadway
Tel: 738 3211

THE RIDGE
3131 Arbutus at 16th
Tel: 738 6311

PACIFIC CINEMATHEQUE
Tel: 688-FILM (688 3456)

Movie Theatres that show first-run Canadian, foreign and art films include:

THE PARK THEATRE
3440 Cambie at 18th
Tel: 876 2747

THE VARSITY
4375 West 10th near Trimble
Tel: 222 2235

Dance

The **Dance Centre** has a hotline, tel: 872 0432.

Classical Music

The Vancouver Symphony Orchestra performs most concerts at the **Orpheum** on Granville Street. There

Theatre

During the summer there are, in addition to the places listed below, two outdoor theatrical venues to consider: **The Bard on the Beach** at Vanier Park features Shakespearean works in a circus tent. The **Theatre under the Stars** in Stanley Park at the Malkin Bowl stages musicals under canvas. Performances at both start at 8.30pm; dress warmly. Tel: 687 0174.

THE VANCOUVER PLAYHOUSE
Queen Elizabeth Theatre
630 Hamilton near Georgia
Tel: 665 3050
This is Vancouver's main stage for both traditional and contemporary theatre.

WATERFRONT THEATRE
Cartwright at Old Bridge
Granville Island
Tel: 685 6217
Look for new works by BC playwrights which tend to be staged at this venue.

ARTS CLUB THEATRE
1585 Johnston Street
Granville Island
Tel: 687 1644
Two professional theatres offer a repertoire that includes a range of plays from hit comedies to passionate human drama.

is a series of free concerts during the summer in the parks, tel: 684 9100.

The Vancouver Opera performs four major works a year at the **Queen Elizabeth Theatre**, 630 Hamilton near Georgia, tel: 683 0222.

Country classics

Clubs and Cabarets

Most clubs become crowded shortly after 10pm. Cover charges are very reasonable, ranging from nothing to $5. Dress codes are enforced where mentioned.

The **Jazz Hotline** can be heard by telephoning 682 0706.

THE COMMODORE BALLROOM
870 Granville Street
Tel: 683 9413
Built in 1929 with a sprung dance floor (it bounces on railcar springs), this 1,000 person dance hall is the best of all possible worlds if your music is headlined. From grunge through rock to swing.

ROXY NIGHTCLUB
932 Granville Street
Tel: 684 7999
This is a fun club with a talented house band that will make you dance. The crowd is mainly student age.

RICHARD'S ON RICHARDS
1036 Richards at Nelson
Tel: 687 6794
A dress code (beyond jeans) dance club for the 30 to 40 year olds.

Loud and live

BIG BAM BOO CLUB
1236 West Broadway
Tel: 733 2220
Ladies night packages, extreme and hot dance parties – reservation required.

BAR NONE
1222 Hamilton in Yaletown
Tel: 689 7000
Live bands, pool tables, beautiful fresh scrubbed people aged 22 to 40.

SHARK CLUB AND GRILL BAR
180 West Georgia
Tel: 681 2211
Combines a popular bar, music and pool tables. Big dance floor and DJs.

TOWN PUMP
66 Water Street
Tel: 683 6695
The best venue for new and established international bands – aternative/roots rock. Expect to pay $10–$20. Advance tickets at TicketMaster.

FAIRVIEW PUB
898 West Broadway
Tel: 872 1262
Jazz and rhythm and blues are the headline entertainments.

MARS RESTAURANT AND CLUB
1320 Richards Street
Tel: 662 7707
Two floors, three bars, intelligent lighting system illuminates DJs offering top forty and retro music.

Calendar of Special Events

JANUARY / FEBRUARY

On New Year's day the **Polar Bear Swim** ushers in the New Year with a splash, when 2,000 stalwarts brave the icy waters of English Bay.

Those who prefer whisky, haggis and poetry may be more tempted to join in the **Scottish Weekend** which celebrates Burns' Night at the end of January in Harrison.

The **Chinese New Year** is celebrated with fireworks, feasts and parades by Vancouver's Chinese population and anyone who wants to join in. Dates vary according to Chinese calendar, tel: 682 2222.

MARCH / APRIL

If you want to see the sea-lions arrive at Steveston jetty, tel: 272 9187 for the arrival date.

This is also the time to visit the **Vancouver Playhouse International Wine Festival** where regional and international wines can be tasted, tel: 872 6622 for details.

In April, Vancouver's Sikh community hold the **Baisahki** parade, a colourful event which ends up at the Sikh temple. There's also the **TerrifVic Jazz Party** and the **Antiques and Collectibles Fair** on Vancouver Island.

MAY

The **Cloverdale Rodeo**, held in late May, offers big prize money to top bronco-riders, steer-wrestlers and calf-ropers, in an event which will make you think you are part of a cowboy movie. Tel: 576 9461.

Vancouver's **Children's Festival** features international performers and storytellers in big-top tents, tel: 687 7697 for information.

Aquatic events include: the **Flatwater Racing Regatta**, Long Beach; **Tea Cup Races**, Inner Harbour; and at Victoria the **Decorated Boat Parade** and **Annual Gorge Regatta**.

Chinese New Year

JUNE / JULY

June sees the **World Championship Cup Dragon Boat Festival**, in the middle of the month at False Creek when 2,000 recreational and competitive paddlers take part in this colourful event, tel: 669 8282.

The **du Maurier Jazz Festival**, with two weeks of jazz starting in late June, is another popular event, tel: 872 5200.

On 1 July, **Canada Day** celebrations are held throughout the province. One of these is the **Gastown Grand Prix bicycle race**.

The **Vancouver Folk Music Festival** at the Jericho beach park, is held in mid-July, tel: 602 9798.

Also in mid-July are the Nanaimo–Vancouver **bathtub race**, an international fireworks competition, Bard on the Beach (Shakespeare in Vanier park), and the Gay/Lesbian Pride parade, tel: 738 4304.

The **Artcraft Festival** is the umbrella name for when Saltspring Island craftspeople gather in Ganges every summer, tel: 537 1186.

AUGUST

The **International Comedy Festival** is held in early August, at Granville Island, tel: 683 0883 for further information.

The August skies light up with the **Symphony of Fire**, a magnificent display of pyrotechnics which can be seen anywhere around the English Bay area, tel: 738 4304.

The **Powell Street Festival** in Oppenheimer Park is the Japanese community fair, tel: 739 9388.

Motor racing enthusiasts flock to the **Indy Vancouver** which offers world-class Indy-car racing at Pacific Place in late August, tel: 661 7223 for details.

SEPTEMBER / OCTOBER

The **Fringe Festival** is an enjoyable and sometimes controversial late-September event, offering small stage alternative theatre and performance art, tel: 257 0350.

Shortly afterwards comes the **Vancouver International Film Festival**, held in early October, tel: 685 0260.

A completely different kind of festival is **Davali** a fascinating Indo-Canadian festival in late October to early November.

Chilliwack and Whistler are the places to go if you want to join in annual **Oktoberfest** celebrations.

Celebrating in style

NOVEMBER / DECEMBER

The **Festival of Lights** in Van Dusen Botanical Gardens sees 19,000 lights switched on in a Christmas spectacular which will delight the whole family, tel: 266 7194.

The **Carol Ships** is an unusual holiday season parade of yachts which takes place at English Bay and Burrard Inlet, tel: 687 9558 for exact dates.

Another event in the pre-Christmas celebrations is the arrival of **Sinter Klaas** by steamboat in New Westminster, tel: 522 6894 for more details. A festival enjoyed by adults as well as children.

Practical Information

GETTING THERE

By Air

Vancouver International Airport is 16km (10 miles) from the downtown area servicing regional (south terminal) and worldwide destinations, particularly the Pacific Rim. An airport levy on departure varies from $5–$15 depending on destination. Taxis to downtown are currently $22. An airport express bus leaves for major hotels every 30 minutes. Travellers with luggage should try to avoid public transportation.

By Rail

The transcontinental train, Via Rail, departs Vancouver three times weekly. In Canada, tel: 1-800-561 8630. In the US, tel: 1-800-665 0200. Amtrak has reintroduced passenger service from Seattle to Vancouver, tel: 1-800-872 7245 for more details.

By Road

From US/Seattle take Interstate 5 north through Canadian customs at Blaine (up to an hour's daytime wait) and follow Highway 99 north into Vancouver. Crossing the Granville Bridge take Seymour north into downtown. From Eastern BC and Canada, Trans-Canada Highway 1 and 1A connects to Vancouver.

By Sea

BC Ferry Corporation operates one of the world's largest, most modern ferry fleets. From Vancouver for ferries to Vancouver Island/Nanaimo and the Sunshine coast take Highway 1A-99 North to the Horseshoe Bay terminal (crowded on summer weekends). For Victoria, South Vancouver Island, the Gulf Islands, and Nanaimo take 1A south to Highway 17 and the Tsawwassen ferry terminal. For 24-hour ferry information tel: 1-888-223 3779. By bus via the BC Ferries Pacific Coach Lines, tel: 1-800-661 1725. Check for high speed catamaran ferries from Vancouver to Victoria and Seattle.

Flying the flags

When to Visit

Vancouver belongs to travellers during the warm, wet summer (June to September). Locals take their vacations in August, and September, wonderful for its Indian summer, is now the most popular month for tourists. Winter's best month is February, the height of the ski season.

Visas and Passports

There are no visa requirements for visitors from the US, Japan, Australia and the UK but passports are necessary. European travellers should verify visa requirements with Canadian consulates in their home country as some restrictions may apply.

Canadian customs

Customs

There are no currency restrictions. Travellers may take advantage of duty-free shopping. For in-depth duty requirements tel: 666 7342.

Weather

Warm Pacific currents bathe Vancouver in mild weather throughout the year, and Vancouver Island shelters the city from Pacific storms. Snow seldom falls, but persistent cloud cover with frequent light rain is the rule between November and May. Summer high temperatures range between 17–25°C (67–80°F), winter temperatures between 5–11°C (41–52°F). For weather reports: Environment Canada, tel: 299 9000 ext. 3500.

Clothing

Casual to casual-dressy is the rule. On summer nights a light sweater or a windbreaker will keep you comfortable. Bring an umbrella and SPF15 sunscreen too as the weather is very changeable. In winter bring raingear and waterproof footwear.

Electricity

120 volts AC.

Time Differences

The city is on Pacific Standard Time, with Daylight Saving Time in effect between early April and late October. Pacific Standard Time is GMT minus 8 hours.

Geography

Vancouver has a coastal rainforest climate. It is surrounded on three sides by water, Burrard Inlet to the north, the Fraser river to the south and the Strait of Georgia between the city and Vancouver Island. The coast mountains rise 3,000m (9,840ft) to the east. Population growth is pressing development into the mountains, but most growth is in the communities of the Fraser river delta to the south and east.

The heart of Vancouver is a peninsula comprising the downtown, the West End and Stanley Park areas. False Creek, a small saltwater inlet, separates downtown from its southern neighbourhoods of Fairview, Kitsilano, West Point Grey and others. To the north across Burrard Inlet at the base of the Coast Range are the residential communities of Vancouver and North Vancouver.

Be prepared!

Government

Vancouver City Council consists of the mayor and 10 aldermen, elected every three years. Victoria is the seat of the provincial legislature, and Vancouver is divided into 10 provincial electoral districts. Representatives are elected from the New Democratic, Social Credit, Liberal and the new Reform parties. Vancouver also elects five members to the federal government of Canada.

Economy

Forestry, mining, international trade, and tourism are key industries, making British Columbia the most volatile economy in Canada. Vancouver is an emergent international financial centre and the largest port in North America in terms of import and export tonnage. Vancouver has also become a major motion picture production centre nicknamed 'Hollywood North'.

Population

Migration from the provinces and immigration from Pacific Rim countries makes Vancouver's 16 percent annual growth rate the second fastest in Canada and the fourth fastest in North America (40,000 people per year).

1996 census information: Vancouver city: 600,000; metropolitan area: 1.9 million. Of this latter figure about 365,000 are of English descent and there are 61 recognized immigrant communities within the city limits. The Chinese community of 200,000 is the largest.

How Not To Offend

Vancouverites are polite and friendly with a touch of English reserve. They are used to sharing their city and will go to unusual lengths to help a visitor. Most Canadians do not appreciate Canada being mistaken for the United States.

MONEY MATTERS

Currency

Canadian money is in dollars and cents. Dollar bills, in denominations of two, five, 10 and 20 are the most common. The one-dollar coin is known as the 'looney', the two-dollar coin the 'tooney'. The value of the Canadian dollar fluctuates in relation to its US counterpart and all world currencies.

Credit Cards and Cheques

Major credit cards and travellers cheques are accepted virtually everywhere. Exchange rates vary widely. Check with foreign exchange offices, located near Georgia and Burrard, or one of 25 foreign banks in the city.

Cash Machines

Cash machines are located in bank foyers and the larger stores. Most US banks are accepted. Many have 24-hour, card-only secure access.

Tipping

Tips are not included in your bills or taxi fares. 15 percent is the norm.

Taxes

A 6 percent provincial sales tax applies to purchases except groceries and books. An additional Goods and Services Tax of 7 percent is added to all purchases except groceries. Foreign visitors may apply for tax refunds on accommodation, and consumer goods for export. Keep receipts and ask for rebate forms at your hotel.

Save the forests

metric and they are strictly enforced by photo radar. Overtime parking tickets are common.

HOURS AND HOLIDAYS

Business Hours

Stores are open daily including Sunday, although some close on Monday. Most open at 10am Monday to Friday but a few open later on weekends. Closing times vary but downtown stores stay open late during the week in summer, and close at 6pm Saturday and Sunday.

Market Days

Granville Island public market: fresh food of every description, crafts and flowers (daily 9am–6pm May to September, closed Monday in winter).

Lonsdale Quay: North Vancouver – shops, crafts and food (daily 9.30am–6.30pm, Friday 9.30am–9pm).

Public Holidays

New Year:	1 January
Good Friday:	date varies
Victoria Day:	3rd Monday in May
Canada Day:	1 July
BC Day:	1st Monday in August
Labour Day:	1st Monday in September
Thanksgiving:	2nd Monday in October
Remembrance Day:	11 November
Christmas Day:	25 December
Boxing Day:	26 December

GETTING AROUND

On Foot

Fifteen kilometres (9 miles) of walking/biking trails give breathtaking views from numerous vantage points along the waterfront from Stanley Park around False Creek to Kitsilano. Don't follow the local habit of stepping out onto a busy street and expecting traffic to stop. If you walk any of the bridges stay by the railings, as bike commuters speed along the inside of the walk. (For bike rentals *see Day 2 Itinerary.*)

Taxis

Hard to flag on a rainy Friday evening, but taxis can be found at hotels and taxistands throughout the city. Rates start at $2.10 and go up $1.21 per kilometre, tax included. Cabs are clean and comfortable.

Bus / SkyTrain

Bus routes and the SkyTrain are commuter-oriented. Block tickets are sold in stores displaying red and blue fare-dealer signs. Transfers are valid for return bus trips within 90 minutes, and valid for the SeaBus and SkyTrain.

Passenger Ferries / SeaBus

The passenger ferry SeaBus leaves the old CPR station at Cordova (due north from Robson Square) for North Vancouver's Lonsdale Quay every 15 minutes until midnight. The diminutive Granville Island ferries make quick jaunts across False Creek from the foot of Thurlow Street downtown.

By Car

Vancouver does not have freeways entering the central business district and traffic jams are a major problem. However, driving is safe and sedate. Speed limits are in

Aquabus travel

ACCOMMODATION

Hotels

Prices in Canadian dollars. $ = $40–$70. $$ = $70–110. $$$ = $110 upwards.

HOTEL VANCOUVER
900 West Georgia Street
Tel: 684 3131 or toll free 1-800-268 9411. Fax: 662 1937
Located in the centre of town, its chateau-style copper roof of green verdigris is the architectural icon of the city. A Canadian Pacific Hotel; high standards of service and amenities including a spa/pool/gym. 508 rooms. $$$

FOUR SEASONS
791 West Georgia at Howe
Tel: 689 9333 or toll free 1-800-332 3442 Fax: 684 4555
One of Vancouver's three Five Diamond AAA/CAA hotel awards. A heritage building, and impeccable service. Home of **Chartwell**, one of Vancouver's best restaurants. 450 rooms. $$$

PAN PACIFIC HOTEL
300–999 Canada Place
Tel: 662 8111 or toll free 1-800-937 1515 Fax: 685 8690
This fabulous dockside hotel near the Canada Place Convention Centre was the choice of the Prince and Princess of Wales

when they visited Vancouver in 1986. Highlights are the great views and the Five Sails seafood restaurant. $$$

SUTTON PLACE HOTEL
845 Burrard Street
Tel: 682 5511 or toll free 1-800-543 4300 Fax: 682 5311
Another Five Diamond rating. Elegant marble and flowers in stately rooms. 444 rooms. $$$. **Gerard Lounge** is very popular with the after-work crowd.

WATERFRONT CENTRE
900 Canada Place at the foot of Howe
Tel: 691 1991 or toll free 1-800-268 9411(Canada); 1-800-828 7447 (US)
Lots of good local art decorates this glass tower. This Canadian Pacific Hotel is the newest in the city with a grand airy entry, generous rooms and suites. Service and amenities are excellent. Just above Burrard Inlet, with harbour views from 75 percent of the rooms. 489 rooms. $$$

Waterfront Centre Hotel

THE BLUE HORIZON
1225 Robson at Butte
Tel: 688 1411 or toll free 1-800-633 1333 Fax: 688 4461
The Blue Horizon's renovated rooms are huge and all have excellent views; the hotel is located between Stanley Park and Robson Square. 214 rooms. $$

THE SYLVIA HOTEL

1154 Gilford at Beach Avenue
Tel: 681 9321
An ivy covered heritage hotel, right on English Bay with the fun of Denman Street nearby, makes this one of the best locations in the city. European style, it is not fancy nor is its service top notch but you are dealing with a legend. 116 rooms. **$**

ATRIUM INN

2889 East Hastings Street
Tel: 254 1000 or toll free 1-800-663 8158
Fax: 253 1234
Famous for its good value. Shuttle bus to downtown, air-conditioned rooms. Conveniently located near all the top 10 tourist attractions. **$$**

Other Accommodation

ENGLISH BAY INN

1968 Comox at Chilco
Tel: 683 8002
Romantic, antique, a classic Tudor guest house with only five guest rooms (each with bathroom and phone). Crystal and china breakfast table, privacy, no smoking, and only a block off the Park and English Bay. **$$**

JOHNSON HOUSE

2278 West 34th Avenue
Tel: 266 4175
Centrally located bed and breakfast inn. Homemade muffins. No smoking, no credit cards. **$$**

PENNY FARTHING INN

2855 West 6th Avenue
Tel: 739 9002
Bed and breakfast inn. Antique furnishings. Some rooms with mountain views. No smoking in the house. **$$**

KENYA COURT GUEST HOUSE

2230 Cornwall in Kitsilano
Tel: 738 7085
A 1920s four-unit guest house across from Kitsilano Beach, with large one- and two-bedroom suites (best views on the 2nd and 3rd floors), a rooftop solarium where a complimentary breakfast is served. No smoking, no credit cards. **$$**

Serious cycling

LOCARNO BEACH BED AND BREAKFAST

West Point Grey
Tel: 731 5942 (Town and Country Bed and Breakfast Registry) for reservations.
Just across from the beginning of the endless beach of Locarno-Jericho-Spanish Banks. No smoking. 3 rooms. **$**

VANCOUVER HOSTEL

1515 Discovery near Fourth
Tel: 224 3208
Fax: 224 4852
A 285-bed dorm with a restaurant and kitchens for self-catering, plus mountain bike rental. In a wonderful setting at Jericho Beach, but far from downtown – 30 minutes on one of the worst transit routes. **$**

OUTDOOR RECREATION

To many Vancouverites being outdoors is the most important thing in their lives. The mountains, beaches, rivers, lakes and ocean have created limitless possibilities for recreation. Here are just a few ideas.

Bicycling: Stanley Park anchors the downtown core with many miles of trails into the heart of the park (*see Day 2 Itinerary*). The Seawall links up with the 15-km (9½-mile) Vancouver Seaside Bicycle Route at the south end of the Park.

Fishing: For salmon: Sewell's Marina, tel: 921 3474, at Horseshoe Bay: supplies for everything from rod and bait to fishing boats.

Golf: Vancouver Parks and Recreation operates three full-length municipal

courses and three pitch and putt courses. The most challenging full-length course is McCleery Golf Course, tel: 257 8191. Other notable city courses open to the public are the University Golf Club at UBC, tel: 224 1818; Mayfair Lakes in Richmond, tel: 276 0505; and Gleneagles in West Vancouver, tel: 921 7353.

Hiking: For the casual and avid hiker Mount Seymour Provincial Park, tel: 986 2261. Alpine meadows and views of the Coast Range and Georgia Strait.

Horseback Riding: For alpine scenery on horseback: Golden Ears Riding Stable, Maple Ridge, tel: 878 4278.

Hot Air Ballooning: balloon rides over the farmlands of the Fraser Valley: Fantasy Balloon Charters, tel: 530 1974.

River Rafting: Some of the most exciting big-water rapids in North America are on the Fraser and Thompson rivers. Contact Hyak Wilderness Adventures, tel: 734 8622.

Sea Kayaking: Ecomarine, tel: 689 7575, operates two rental outlets on Granville Island and Jericho Beach, suitable for novices and experienced paddlers.

Tennis: The city Parks and Recreation Department operates 175 courts (free) throughout the city. Six courts in Stanley Park can be reserved, tel: 257 8400.

Sea kayaking

Windsurfing: Jericho Sailing Centre is the best for this sport. Try also Windsure Windsurfing, tel: 224 4177, for rentals and lessons.

HEALTH AND EMERGENCIES

Pharmacies

Shoppers' Drug Mart at Davie and Thurlow is open 24 hours, tel: 685 6445. There are numerous pharmacies.

Medical / Dental Services

Visitors in need of a doctor or dentist on weekdays may attend drop-in clinics at the Medicentre (tel: 683 8138) or Dentacentre (tel: 669 6700), both in the Bentall Centre at Burrard and Dunsmuir. At other times Vancouver General Hospital emergency is the quickest way to get medical attention. Visitors are advised to have insurance to cover costs.

Crime / Trouble

Tourists have little to fear in Vancouver. Night-time walking in most areas downtown is safe and popular, though street drugs are a worsening problem. Theft from cars is a problem; don't leave items visible in an unattended vehicle. Tel: 911 from any telephone for police, fire or ambulance.

COMMUNICATIONS

Post

Canada Post offices are found throughout the city, but people often use mini-outlets in convenience stores and pharmacies. Look for Canada Post shingles on buildings and in store windows. Hours vary and service is often available at weekends.

Telephone

The country code for Canada is 1. The two area codes covering British Columbia are 604 and 250. Dial 0 for operator assistance and 411 for information.

Media

The afternoon *Vancouver Sun* and the morning *Province* are the local dailies though each takes a day off: the *Sun* on Sunday and the *Province* on Saturday.

There are 12 community papers. The *Georgia Straight*, published each Thursday, is the best free compendium of issues and events. *Vancouver* magazine is a good city monthly. There are eight local TV channels and 20 radio stations. The Canadian Broadcasting Company's CBC 93.1 FM 690 AM is one of the finest ways to get to know Canada. Best in-town newsstand for out of town news: **Mayfair News**, 1535 W. Broadway off Granville, tel: 738 8951. In the hotel and business district: **Manhattan Books**, 1089 Robson off Thurlow, tel: 681 9074, specializes in periodicals and French titles.

USEFUL INFORMATION

People with disabilities will find that Vancouver is a wheelchair-friendly city, and wheelchair users are active. The stop lights 'chirp' for the sight impaired at some crossings.

Children

With so many people living downtown, well mannered drivers and good natured people, it's a kids' city. Itineraries of particular interest to kids: *Day 2* with Stanley Park's wading pools, water parks, miniature train, zoo and aquarium; *Day 3* with Granville Island and its water park, lawns, boats, and kids-only market. And the *Morning of the Future*'s Science World is made for kids. For child care, contact Neighbourhood Babysitters, tel: 737 2248; Over the Rainbow Drop-In Playcare Centre, tel: 683 2624.

ATTRACTIONS

UBC Museum of Anthropology, 6393 N.W. Marine Drive (at UBC), tel: 822 3825 (Tuesday 11am–9pm, Wednesday to Monday 11am–5pm; closed Monday in winter). First Nations Pacific Northwest culture (*see Day 3 Itinerary*).

Vancouver Art Gallery, 750 Hornby Street at Robson, tel: 662 4700 (Monday, Wednesday, Friday, Saturday 10am–5pm, Thursday 10am–9pm, Sunday noon–5pm). Canadian artist Emily Carr and regular visiting exhibitions (*see Day 1 Itinerary*).

The Lookout at Harbour Centre, 555 West Hastings Street, tel: 689 0421. A 360° birds-eye view located in the heart of the city.

Lynn Canyon Park and Suspension Bridge, 3663 Park Road North Vancouver, tel: 981 3103. Free. A beautiful forest park with its canyon rapid spanned by a 72-m (240-ft) suspension bridge.

Grouse Mountain Skyride, North Vancouver, tel: 984 0661. A gondola ride to the top of Grouse Mountain (*see North Shore Itinerary*).

Reifel Migratory Bird Sanctuary, Highway 17 turn-off from 99 south, tel: 946 6980 (daily 9am–4pm). Thousands of migratory birds visit this reserve located in the marshes of the Fraser river estuary.

SPORTS

Spectator Sports

Baseball: The Triple-A Vancouver Canadians play ball througout the summer at Nat Bailey Stadium, a classic minor-league field often compared with Fenway Park in Boston, tel: 299 9000 ext. 2255.

Hockey: The Vancouver Canucks of the National Hockey League play the world's fastest game at the Pacific Coliseum from October through May, tickets from TicketMaster, tel: 299 9000 ext. 3055.

Football: The BC Lions play in the Canadian Football League, US-style

A whale of a time

Football stadium

game. For information tel: 299 9000 ext. 3355.

Horse Racing: Thoroughbred racing takes place nightly at Exhibition Park. For race times, tel: 299 9000 ext. 7223.

USEFUL ADDRESSES / NUMBERS

Vancouver Travel Infocentre Waterfront Centre, 200 Burrard Street (at Cordova), tel: 683 2000. An additional Vancouver Travel Infocentre booth operates during the summer in the Pacific Centre Mall at Robson and Hornby (Monday to Saturday 9am–5pm, Sunday noon–5pm).

Tourism BC, tel: 685 0032 for detailed information on just about anything, anywhere.

BC Parks, Parliament Buildings, Victoria BC, V8V 1X5.

BC Coalition of People with Disabilities, 204-456 W Broadway, Vancouver V5Y IR3, tel: 875 0188.

FURTHER READING

Insight Guide: Vancouver & Surroundings, Insight Guides, London, 1999. Comprehensive and readable guide to the city and region illustrated with excellent photographs.

Exploring Vancouver, by Robin Ward, Hal Kelman, Ron Phillips, UBC Press, 1993. Covers the city's best, worst and unique architecture with outstanding photographs.

Vancouver, A City Album, edited by Anne Kloppenborg et al, Douglas and McIntyre, Vancouver, 1991. An historical photo album with excerpts from the archives and press of the day.

Vancouver and Its Region, edited by Graeme Wynn and Timothy Oke, UBC

Press, Vancouver, 1992. Essays on the physical and socio-economic evolution of Vancouver.

Vancouver, a Visual History, by Bruce Macdonald, Talon Books, Vancouver, 1992. If there's one book that every city should have and every visitor should buy, it's this one. A decade by decade, map by map history of the city.

Green Spaces of Vancouver, by Anne Templeman-Klut, Brighouse Press, Vancouver, 1990. Information on hiking routes.

Beyond the Island: An Illustrated History of Victoria, by Peter A Baskerville. Windsor Publications, 1986.

Banners and Bands: A Guide to the Festivals of the Pacific Northwest, by Eileen Marrett. Upper Case Publishing, 1991.

Guidebook to Ethnic Vancouver, by Ann Petrie. Hancock House, 1982.

Vancouver's emblem

The Vancouver Trivia Book, by Craig O Henderson. Polestar Press, 1985.

Saltwater City, An Illustrated History of the Chinese in Vancouver, by Paul Yee. Douglas and McIntyre, 1988.

Easy Hiking Around Vancouver, by Jean Cousins and Heather Robinson. Douglas and McIntyre, 1990.

109 Walks in British Columbia's Lower Mainland, by Mary and David Macaree. Douglas and McIntyre, 1990.

Bicycling Greater Vancouver and the Gulf Islands, by Maggie Burtinshaw and Mary Ellen Bradshaw. Gordon Soules Publishing, 1990.

Vancouver, by Pat Kramer. An Altitude Superguide, 1999.

The keeper of the light

ACKNOWLEDGMENTS

Photography Joel W Rogers *and*

13T City of Vancouver Archives
72, 73T, 74 Jack C M Wong
12, 13B, 14, 15 Stanley Young/Vancouver Public Library

Handwriting V Barl
Cover Design Klaus Geisler
Cartography Lovell Johns
Production Editor Stuart A. Everitt